Innovation und Entrepreneurship

Innovative Konzepte und unternehmerische Leistungen sind für Wohlstand und Fortschritt von entscheidender Bedeutung. Diese Schriftenreihe vereint wissenschaftliche Arbeiten zu diesem Themenbereich. Sie beschreiben substanzielle Erkenntnisse auf hohem methodischen Niveau.
Innovative concepts and entrepreneurial performance are crucial for prosperity and progress. This publication series brings together scientific contributions on these topics. They describe substantial findings at a high methodological level.

More information about this series at http://www.springer.com/series/12264

Stefan Nothelfer

Behavior in Foreign Languages

Experimental Evidence on Creativity, Cooperation, and Culture-Related Effects

Springer Gabler

Stefan Nothelfer
Berlin, Germany

D 19 Dissertation Center for Digital Technology & Management, LMU Munich, and Max Planck Institute for Innovation and Competition

ISSN 2627-1168 ISSN 2627-1184 (electronic)
Innovation und Entrepreneurship
ISBN 978-3-658-31852-9 ISBN 978-3-658-31853-6 (eBook)
https://doi.org/10.1007/978-3-658-31853-6

Responsible Editor: Carina Reibold
This Springer Gabler imprint is published by the registered company Springer Fachmedien Wiesbaden GmbH part of Springer Nature.
The registered company address is: Abraham-Lincoln-Str. 46, 65189 Wiesbaden, Germany

Foreword

In this dissertation, Stefan Nothelfer enters uncharted waters to investigate the influence of foreign language use on behavior, particularly focusing on creativity, cooperation, and culture-related effects. His research contributes to our understanding of human behavior and spans bridges between the largely disciplinary silos of behavioral economics and psychology.

The dissertation focuses on the impact of foreign language use on innovation processes. Innovators often work and interact in a foreign language. Multinational firms frequently have international teams in research and development, and the technology world relies heavily on international talent. Entrepreneurs and startups tend to use English as their lingua franca, even when based entirely in non-English-speaking countries. Hence, the relevance of this research is immediately apparent. With its focus on creativity and cooperation, the thesis targets two important aspects of innovators' behavior.

In his first essay, Stefan Nothelfer disentangles potential effects of foreign language use and introduces a sophisticated experimental design to distinguish between language- or culture-specific effects, cultural accommodation, and general foreign language effects. The findings challenge previously reported findings of cultural accommodation and foreign language effects.

In the second essay, the book draws on a large international laboratory experiment of language-induced effects on creativity. By recombining established and innovative measures of creativity, the study builds and analyzes a unique dataset comprising 13,842 ratings of 2,307 creative products. The results substantially enrich the empirical foundations regarding the interplay between language and creativity.

In the third essay, the thesis explores cooperation and expected cooperation in foreign language settings. The use of a well-established game to measure cooperation under different language combinations ensures comparability with previous studies. Results point towards the presence of language- or culture-specific effects and underline the need to differentiate these from general foreign language effects.

The empirical foundation of these essays is an international series of laboratory and online experiments in three languages. A particular advantage of the data is the cross-pairing of combinations of mother tongues and treatment languages across comparable subject pools in different countries. Stefan Nothelfer's work includes creating a custom-built mobile laboratory which allowed him to conduct experiments at nine universities in three countries.

All three essays enrich the discussion of language and behavior in general and confirm the importance of language as a key aspect of the behavioral foundations of innovation. I strongly recommend this volume to scholars from management, psychology, or behavioral economics, as well as anyone interested in innovative experimental research, cross-cultural teams, linguistic relativity, and creativity.

Prof. Dietmar Harhoff, Ph.D.

Acknowledgements

This work would not have been possible without the wonderful support of colleagues, mentors, and friends.

First and foremost, I would like to thank Dietmar Harhoff for his continuous support. His trust, willingness to support unconventional research projects, financial support and valuable advice were the basis for this work.

I thank my co-author Marco Kleine for numerous hours of insightful and fun discussions, honing experimental designs, and hands-on operational support. Without his methodological expertise and continuous commitment, this project would not exist.

Moreover, I would like to thank Martin Spann for taking on the role as my second advisor at the Ludwig-Maximilians-Universität.

A particular thank you goes to my friends and colleagues at the Center for Digital Technology and Management, a true home for ideas: Laura Bechthold, Gesa Biermann, Patrick Bilic, Patrick Christ, Michael Chromik, Fabian Dany, Maximilian Engelken, Florian Gall, Veronika Gamper, Claudius Jablonka, Florian Korte, Till Kröger, Florian Lachner, Kilian Moser, Philipp Nägelein, Benedikt Römer, Tom Schelo, Uta Weber, and Stefanie Weniger. All the excellent discussions over coffee and lunch, legendary foosball matches, countless social gatherings and long office nights will stay in fond memory.

Likewise, I thank my friends and colleagues at the Max Planck Institute of Innovation and Competition: Stefano Baruffaldi, Lorenz Brachtendorf, Dennis Byrski, Nadine Chochoiek, Fabian Gaessler, Jonas Heite, Frank Mueller-Langer, Felix Pöge, Zhaoxin Pu, Myriam Rion, Michael Rose, Laura Rosendahl-Huber, Matthias Schmitt, Stefan Sorg, Gisela Stingl, Magdalena Streicher, Roland Stürz, and Alexander Suyer. I appreciate the great team spirit and their support has been of high value to this project. Special thanks go to the MPI laboratory, IT and administrative teams, as well as to all research assistants, who went the extra mile for enabling the mobile laboratory. In particular, I would like to thank Cecilie Classen, Natalie Eisenhut, Andreas Kraus, and Weile Weng for handling all technical and operational challenges brilliantly.

The data collection would not have been possible without the selfless support of partners at various universities. Thank you, Bernard Banoun, Sarah Buschfeld, Franziska Günther, Florian Henke, Britta Jallerat-Jabs, Alexander Kautzsch, Céline Largier, Hans-Jürgen Lüsebrink, Jeanne Schueller, Carmen Taleghani-Nikazm, Céline Trautmann-Waller, Hélène Vinckel-Roisin, and Arlette Warken.

During the dissertation I was able to spend some fruitful time as visiting scholar at Columbia University. I am very grateful to Eli Noam and would like to thank him for being such an outstanding host.

With special appreciation I thank Maike Wiehmeier for all her love and positive spirit. You make me a better person and I am fortunate to have you in my life.

In closing, I would like to express my deepest gratitude to my family for their unconditional support, love, and for being the wonderful humans they are. This dissertation is dedicated to my parents Christa and Hans.

Stefan Nothelfer

Contents

List of Figures

List of Tables

1 Introduction and Overview

1.1 Motivation

There are more than 7000 living languages in the world (Simons & Fenning, 2018). This enormous linguistic diversity stands in stark contrast to the handful of languages that are mainly used to interact in the business world, international politics, and academia. A large share of the world's population frequently works and interacts in foreign languages, and a large share of important decisions are made in foreign language settings.

English has become the lingua franca of the international business world (Neeley, 2012). By the end of 2017, 18 of 30 German DAX corporations had changed their official language to English (Obmann, 2017). As a consequence, internal communication and documentation take place in a language that large parts of the workforce have encountered for the first time in middle school. Regular use of foreign languages stretches far beyond the business world. Important policy decisions are commonly worked out in foreign language settings, as most international organizations have agreed upon a fixed set of few procedural languages (see, e.g., European Commission, 2013; United Nations, 2018). On an international level, scientific knowledge is mostly shared in English, and this dissertation is a perfect example of research in a foreign language setting. With an increasingly globalized and digital world, foreign language processing has furthermore become part of many people's everyday life. More than 50% of the world's websites are written in English (W3Techs, 2018), while less than 5% of the world's population is of English mother tongue.

S. Nothelfer, *Behavior in Foreign Languages*, Innovation und Entrepreneurship, https://doi.org/10.1007/978-3-658-31853-6_1

Given the ongoing globalization and increasing digitization of societies, foreign language use is likely to become an even more common phenomenon in the near future.[1]

All this raises a fundamental question: Does working and interacting in foreign languages affect human behavior? Taking into account the widespread use of foreign languages, our knowledge of its effects on behavior is surprisingly limited.

This thesis sets out to expand our knowledge of how foreign language use may influence behavior, with a particular focus on creativity and cooperation. It contributes to research both methodologically and empirically with comprehensive experimental studies. Substantial parts of this work take a behavioral and experimental economics perspective. Yet, this dissertation is basic research on fundamental patterns of human behavior and attempts to bridge disciplinary silos. It is situated at the interface between management science, social psychology, and economics. Within management science, effects of foreign language use are likely to be of relevance for areas such as international business in markets of different languages, cross-linguistic teamwork within firms, and firm-internal language policies. In behavioral economics, research on foreign language effects contributes to a better understanding of human decision-making. Previous research on behavioral effects of foreign language use has been predominantly conducted by social psychologists, and creativity is a central domain of psychology.

1.2 Literature and Background

Several empirical studies report effects of using a foreign language on aspects of human behavior. Foreign language use *per se*, independent of a particular language, has been reported to influence behavior in several domains. For example, it reduces biases in risky decision making (Keysar, Hayakawa, & An, 2012; Costa et al., 2014a) and induces a shift from deontological towards utilitarian decision making in moral dilemmas (Corey et al., 2017; Hayakawa et al., 2017). Moreover, using a foreign language reduces emotional resonance (e.g., Pavlenko, 2005; Dewaele, 2004; 2010) and may blunt intuition (Hayakawa et al., 2017; Costa et al., 2014b).

[1] Mid and long-term future of the world's linguistic diversity and foreign language use seem more uncertain. On the one hand, our world is becoming increasingly globalized, which should promote foreign language use and drive linguistic consolidation. On the other hand, technologies for automated simultaneous translations are on the rise (see, e.g., Brynjolfsson & McAfee, 2004; Brynjolfsson, Hui, & Liu, 2018), potentially leading to a decrease of foreign language use and counterbalancing the consolidation pressure.

Moreover, three theories predict *language-specific* effects on behavior. These theories, outlined below, link individual characteristics of languages or associated cultures to behavior and, therefore, depend on particular combinations of foreign language and mother tongue.

Perhaps most prominent is the concept of linguistic relativity, which is widely attributed to the works of Wilhelm von Humboldt, Franz Boas, Edward Sapir, and Benjamin Whorf (see, e.g., Pütz & Verspoor, 2000; Penn, 2014). Language and thought are regarded as deeply interlocked and inseparable. Different linguistic conceptualizations, for example of time, space, or color, in languages are assumed to impact thought and behavior (see, e.g., Kay & Kempton, 1984; Boroditsky, 2001; 2003). In a foreign language context, I consider linguistic relativity as a possible mechanism for language-induced changes in behavior.

The theories of cultural accommodation and ethnic affirmation are based on cultural differences in behavior. Cultural accommodation assumes that individuals, when using a foreign language, adapt their behavior to the culture they associate with that language (Earle, 1969; Bond & Yang, 1982; Akkermans, Harzing, & van Witteloostuijn, 2010). Accordingly, it predicts behavioral changes towards the typical behavior of the associated culture. Ethnic affirmation predicts the opposite. The theory assumes that foreign language use increases the salience of an individual's own culture, inducing behavioral changes away from the typical behavior of the associated culture (Yang & Bond, 1982; Church, Katigbak, & Castaneda, 1988).

Given these theories and empirical findings, foreign language use may affect multiple domains of human behavior. Yet, our knowledge about the role of foreign language use is far from comprehensive. Existent theories stand in parallel and, due to methodological limitations, large parts of the literature are unable to differentiate between different effect types. More importantly, we know very little about the relevance of potential language-induced effects. Scope, boundaries, and size of effects are mostly unknown and underlying mechanisms are subject to debate (see, e.g., Hayakawa et al., 2017; Akkermans et al., 2010; Corey et al., 2017; Costa et al., 2014a). By focusing on creativity and cooperation, this thesis addresses two behavioral domains that have received little attention with regards to foreign language use, despite their importance.

Creativity is vital to our working world, be it for the development of new products and services, process improvements, general problem-solving, or entrepreneurship (see, e.g., Runco, 1994; 2007; Dosi, 1988; Duncker & Lees, 1945; Ward, 2004). In business, the creativity of individual employees, customers, and suppliers is required to drive innovation (see, e.g., Amabile 1988; 1996; West & Anderson, 1996). Moreover, science relies heavily on creativity (see, e.g., Simonton, 2004), and the arts can be regarded as expressions of creativity (see, e.g., Csikszentmihalyi & Getzels, 1971).

Human cooperation is a fundamental trait in social systems that has been researched extensively (see, e.g., Ledyard, 1995; Dawes & Thaler, 1988; Fehr & Schmidt, 1999; Zelmer, 2003). Cooperation across languages and cultures shapes our globalized world (see, e.g., Dorrough & Glöckner, 2016) and is crucial for international politics, international business, science, or organizations with cross-national teams. Given that cooperation is strongly influenced by communication (see, e.g., Ostrom & Walker, 1991; Ostrom, Walker, & Gardner, 1992), language may play an important part in cooperative behavior.

1.3 Research Approach

This dissertation examines potential language-induced effects in three essays, each corresponding to one chapter. Chapter 2 discusses and compares theories to derive requirements and limitations of empirical research on foreign language effects. Furthermore, the chapter contains an explorative empirical part to search for cultural accommodation, ethnic affirmation, and general foreign language effects. Chapters 3 and 4 are joint work with Marco Kleine. Chapter 3 extends research on foreign language effects to the field of creativity, and chapter 4 investigates the role of foreign language use on cooperation.

At the core of this dissertation stands a series of international laboratory experiments allowing for causal inferences from observed behavior. The empirical analyses of all three chapters make use of these experiments. Participants were randomly assigned to process a given series of tasks in either their mother tongue (control) or in a foreign language (treatment). Additional text reproduction tasks strengthened the language prime. In order to ensure comparable environmental conditions across all locations of the data collection, I have specifically developed and built a novel mobile laboratory with tablet devices and self-sufficient technical infrastructure. Specifications of the mobile laboratory systems are described in detail in Appendix D.

Obtaining suitable subjects for the experiments across different languages has proven to be a particular challenge, as standard subject pools in laboratories usually lack the necessary knowledge of foreign languages. In close collaboration with language departments at seven universities in three countries, I recruited language students as subjects. Apart from having the required proficiency in foreign languages of interest, subject pools of university-level language students are to some degree comparable, which allows drawing some inferences on potential cultural differences (see, e.g., Gächter, Hermann, & Thöni, 2010). More importantly, comparisons within language pairings (e.g., German students of French and French students of German who randomly process in either French or German) permit a methodologically rigorous analysis.

The experiments took place in France (Université Paris-Sorbonne, Université Sorbonne Nouvelle), Germany (Ludwig-Maximilians-Universität München, Universität Regensburg, Universität des Saarlandes), and in the United States (The Ohio State University, University of Wisconsin–Madison). The corresponding languages English, French, and German are frequently used as foreign languages and are highly relevant to the professional world. The study on creativity includes additional web-based sessions to rate creative products. Rating sessions were conducted with subjects from standard laboratory pools in the same countries as the experiment in collaboration with Université Catholique de Lille and Florida State University. I collected data from 469 language students in 59 laboratory sessions, and 312 raters provided a total of 13842 ratings for 2307 creative products online. The resulting dataset contributes significantly to the empirical basis for research on language-induced effects on behavior. To my knowledge, it is one of very few datasets with language pairings across three languages.

1.4 Summary

This dissertation consists of three essays that are outlined in the following paragraphs. The chapters are self-contained and can be read separately. Each chapter includes an own introduction and appendix, while references are jointly listed at the end of this thesis. Appendix D provides technical information on the newly built mobile laboratory, which played a decisive role in the research endeavor. An overarching conclusion and outlook are provided at the end of this thesis.

Chapter 2: In Search of Cultural Accommodation, Ethnic Affirmation, and Foreign Language Effects

The second chapter of this dissertation focuses on theories about language-induced effects on behavior and includes a corresponding explorative empirical analysis. In the first section, I discuss and compare different overlapping theories around language-induced effects on behavior. Potential effects are disentangled and distinguished from each other in graphical and logical representations. A simple model that accounts for general foreign language effects and cultural accommodation/ethnic affirmation is introduced to derive requirements and limitations for empirical designs that target language-induced effects on behavior.

In the subsequent explorative empirical analysis, data from 417[2] participants of the international experimental series is analyzed in search of empirical support for the previously discussed theories of cultural accommodation, ethnic affirmation, and general foreign language effects. The dataset covers the behavioral domains of creativity, aesthetics, self-assessments, cooperation, and cheating.

My findings contradict the theories of cultural accommodation and ethnic affirmation, as the observed patterns of cultural differences and language-induced effects mostly differ from the theories' predictions. In addition, I observe no overarching foreign language effect across the behavioral domains. However, I observe a positive foreign language effect on self-ratings that is moderated by abroad experience (i.e., having lived in a country of the foreign language). Subjects without abroad experience rate self-made illustrations of objects significantly higher on creativity, technical aspects, and aesthetic appeal when processing in a foreign language, compared to processing in their mother tongue. This effect is not observable for subjects with abroad experience. Moreover, foreign language use tends to affect expectations regarding cooperation of others positively.

The chapter contributes to theory by disentangling potentially overlapping effects of foreign language use. Moreover, it contributes methodologically by deriving possibilities and limitations for empirical studies and providing a framework for experimental designs. My empirical results deepen our knowledge about the relevance of cultural accommodation and ethnic affirmation and challenge previous findings.

Chapter 3: Foreign Language Effects on Creativity

In chapter 3, joint work with Marco Kleine, we investigate the impact of foreign language use on creativity, with a particular focus on general foreign language effects. The theory part of this chapter links creativity theory with effects of foreign language use, deriving the working hypothesis of a negative foreign language effect on creativity. This first hypothesis is based on a presumed reduction of emotional resonance[3] and inhibited retrieval of episodic memory[4] when processing in

[2]52 participants with several mother tongues or a mother tongue that was neither English, French, or German had to be excluded from analysis.

[3]i.e., emotional reactions are weakened in a foreign language setting (see, e.g. Dewaele, 2004; 2010; Pavlenko, 2005)

[4]Explicit memory can be subdivided into episodic and semantic memory. Episodic memory stores events and experiences and is believed to be more easily retrieved when the linguistic environment of the storage matches the linguistic environment of retrieval. Semantic memory stores general facts and is believed to be independent of the linguistic context. (see Bartolotti and Marian, 2013)

a foreign language. In a second hypothesis, we account for potential language-specific effects caused by cultural accommodation or ethnic affirmation, which may overlap with general foreign language effects.

Our hypotheses are tested empirically with data from 430[5] participants of the international experimental series and with complementing web-based ratings. Creative performance is measured with creative products from an incentivized real effort task in which subjects illustrated objects of their choice with a given set of material. The particular task was inspired by Laske and Schröder (2017), while we rely on Amabile's (1996) consensual assessment technique for measuring creative performance. Our 430 participants have created 2307 illustrations that were rated by 312 raters in France, the U.S., and Germany. Each illustration was rated by six raters, resulting in a dataset with 13842 creativity ratings as observations.

In our analysis, we find no support for a general foreign language effect on creativity. Moreover, we observe language-specific effects that cannot be attributed to theories of cultural accommodation or ethnic affirmation. In our study, participants of French mother tongue, who process in German, are overall significantly more creative than participants of French mother tongue who process in French. This effect loses significance when we analyze only the most creative products of each participant, indicating that the language-specific effect may not affect participants' maximum creativity.

To our knowledge, this is the first study that examines the impact of foreign language use on creativity and can disentangle foreign language effects from other language-specific effects. The study extends our knowledge of boundaries and relevance of foreign language effects to the important field of creativity. Furthermore, it contributes to creativity research across countries and cultures with a large sample of creative products.

Chapter 4: Cooperation in Foreign Languages

Chapter 4 is joint work with Marco Kleine. We investigate the impact of foreign language processing on human cooperation. The existing body of literature on the role of foreign language use for cooperation and social dilemmas is scarce and raises methodological concerns, predominantly due to a lack of language pairings and language variation. Our study takes a methodologically rigorous approach and enlarges the empirical basis with additional languages and pairings.

We first derive a hypothesis of a negative effect of foreign language use on cooperation from theories of language-induced effects and behavior in social

[5] 39 Participants whose mother tongue structure prevented a random assignment to either the treatment or the control group were excluded from analysis.

dilemmas. Presumed mechanisms are a reduced type 1 processing[6], reduced emotional resonance, and limited access to memory and norms. Our hypothesis is put to the test in a one-shot continuous prisoner's dilemma (Wahl & Nowak, 1999). Furthermore, we elicit expectations of behavior to identify possible drivers behind the hypothesized effects. Our dataset comprises cooperation decisions and expectations from language students who participated in the international experimental series.

Results do not support a general foreign language effect on cooperation and cannot be explained by standard theories of language-induced effects on behavior. However, we do find evidence for language-specific effects, and suggestive evidence for a possible moderating role of abroad experience. Participants of German mother tongue who process the task in French are on average more cooperative than participants of German mother tongue who process in German. Furthermore, having lived in a country of the foreign language seems to affect the language-induced effects. For participants with such abroad experience, we observe a positive effect of foreign language use on cooperation that is primarily driven by subjects of the French-German language pairing. The effect is absent for participants without abroad experience. Additionally, foreign language use tends to increase expectation towards the cooperative behavior of the other player. The overall patterns of expectation and cooperative behavior are not congruent, which indicates that the language-specific effects on cooperation cannot be entirely attributed to changed expectations.

The study improves our understanding of cooperation in foreign language settings and shows the boundaries of foreign language effects. It challenges previously reported findings of cultural accommodation in social dilemmas and demonstrates the importance of investigating multiple paired languages for future research. To our knowledge, we have conducted the first empirical study with language pairings on language-induced effects on cooperation. The observed language-specific effects are an interesting phenomenon and a promising starting point for future research.

[6]Kahneman's (e.g., 2003; 2011) dual process theory of cognition distinguishes between intuitive, fast and automatic processing (type 1), and slower, deliberate processing with conscious judgments (type 2).

In Search of Cultural Accommodation, Ethnic Affirmation, and Foreign Language Effects

2

2.1 Introduction

A large part of the world frequently works and interacts in foreign languages. Yet, research on how processing in foreign languages might affect our thinking and behavior is surprisingly scarce. Several theories state potential behavioral effects of using a language that is different from one's mother tongue. The concept of linguistic relativity links behavior directly to language structures and vocabulary (e.g., Kay & Kempton, 1984, Boroditsky, 2001; Chen, 2013). Cultural accommodation and ethnic affirmation derive effects of foreign language use from cultural differences (e.g., Yang & Bond, 1980; Earle, 1969; Church, Katigbak, & Castaneda, 1988; Bond & Yang, 1982), and recent research indicates that cognitive processing in a foreign language may affect behavior per se, independent of the particular language (e.g. Keysar, Hayakawa, & An, 2012; Costa et al., 2014a; Hayakawa et al., 2017). However, there is no unified theory about language-induced effects on behavior. Existing theories stand largely in parallel and are subject to overlaps. This fragmentation is reflected in empirical research on the role of foreign language use, which often refers to only one of the theories and disregards alternative explanations.

This paper sets out to provide a clear overview of different possible language effects and searches for empirical evidence in favor of or against the main theories discussed in the literature. Its contribution to research is threefold: First, it strengthens theory by comparing, merging, and sharpening existing theories, discussing overlaps and differences. Second, it paves the way for future empirical work on the role of language use by clearly deriving possibilities, limitations, and requirements for empirical research, taking into account several possible effects. Third,

S. Nothelfer, *Behavior in Foreign Languages*, Innovation und Entrepreneurship,
https://doi.org/10.1007/978-3-658-31853-6_2

it explores experimental data from three experiments, searching for convergent patterns that are predicted by the different theories.

The comprehensive dataset has been collected from 417 participants at seven universities in France, Germany, and the U.S. in a series of behavioral experiments. It contains data from seven cross-paired combinations of mother tongue and processing language, allowing to differentiate between different effects. The analysis searches for potential effects within, as well as across four different domains of human behavior, namely creative performance, aesthetics, cooperation, and cheating.

Findings are overall not in line with predictions of the theories of cultural accommodation and ethnic affirmation. While parts of the data indicate no cultural differences in behavior between subject pools, behavioral domains with clear cultural differences show patterns that contradict the two culture-related concepts. Additionally, I observe individual language-specific effects that cannot be attributed to any of the discussed theories.

Furthermore, results indicate no overarching general foreign language effect across all of the observed domains. However, the data support a possible positive foreign language effect on the expected cooperative behavior of others. Furthermore, a foreign language effect that is moderated by abroad experience can be observed on self-ratings around creative performance and aesthetics. Participants without abroad experience (i.e., having lived in a country of the foreign language) who processed in a foreign language rated their products significantly better, compared to participants who processed in their mother tongue. This effect is absent for participants with abroad experience.

The paper is structured as follows. After a summary of existing theories and corresponding empirical research, challenges for research on language-induced effects on behavior are identified. In particular, theoretical arguments are made on the relationship between language and culture, on the baseline of "typical" behavior for a culture, and on possible asymmetries in cultural accommodation or ethnic affirmation. Based on this work, potential effects are disentangled with a graphical illustration and logical representation. Implications for experimental research designs are then derived from modeling potential effects in a system of linear equations. In the explorative empirical part of the paper, I analyze three experiments in search of potential language-induced effects. The paper ends with a discussion of findings, limitations, and possible directions for future research.

2.2 Theories and Previous Research

At least four different theories conceptualize an influence of language use on behavior. The theories of linguistic relativity, cultural accommodation, and ethnic accommodation can be categorized as *language-specific*, as characteristics of specific languages or associated cultures are attributed with influencing behavior. Differences in languages themselves or cultural differences are regarded as the origin for differences in behavior when processing in different languages. Apart from language-specific effects, a *language-independent* effect, merely caused by processing in a language different from one's mother tongue(s), may influence behavior.

Linguistic relativity, which is often referred to as the Sapir-Whorf Hypothesis, assumes that language determines thought and behavior (Kay & Kempton 1984). Grammatical structures and lexica may reflect different conceptualizations of aspects of reality, such as time, shapes, space, or color. These different conceptualizations are believed to influence thought and result in systematically different behavior when people use different languages. (e.g., Boroditsky, 2003; 2001; Everett, 2013; Chen, 2013; Anthanasopoulos & Aveledo, 2013). Linguistic relativity is mainly discussed across different mother tongues and not in the context of foreign language use. However, as behavior is directly linked to language structures, it may apply to foreign language use as well.

While the theory of linguistic relativity relies on systematic differences between *languages*, the theories of cultural accommodation and ethnic affirmation rely on systematic differences between *cultures*, without making explicit assumptions about language structures or vocabularies.

Cultural accommodation assumes that language use triggers associations with a culture that people link to a language. Based on systematic behavioral differences across cultures, cultural accommodation refers to an adaption process. Cultural accommodation predicts that, when using a foreign language, people change their behavior towards the typical behavior of the culture they associate with that language (e.g., Earle, 1969; Church, Katigbak, & Castaneda, 1988; Bond & Yang, 1982; Akkermans, Harzing, & van Witteloostuijn, 2010).

Ethnic affirmation postulates an opposite effect: Using a foreign language is thought to increase the salience of one's own culture, resulting in a behavior that is more typical for one's own culture (Yang & Bond, 1980; Bond & Yang, 1982; Church et al., 1988). Ethnic affirmation and cultural accommodation are in general mutually exclusive. Nevertheless, both could potentially exist in different domains. Bond and Yang (1982) identify commitment as a moderator and argue that ethnic affirmation explains behavior in areas characterized by a high degree of commitment, whereas cultural accommodation is in place in areas with a low degree of commitment.

Systematic changes in behavior that are independent of the particular language and cultural background are subject to research and discussion. Such general *foreign language effects* are explained with differences in psychological distance (Corey et al., 2017) or cognitive processing when using a foreign language, such as an induced switch from intuitive towards deliberate processing (Cipolletti, McFarlane, & Weissglass 2016; Urbig et al., 2016), blunted intuition (Hayakawa et al., 2017), or a reduced emotional resonance (Keysar, Hayakawa, & An, 2012; Costa et al., 2014a).

To a large extent, empirical research on the impact of language on behavior mirrors the landscape of corresponding theories. The four theories stand mostly in parallel and are rarely all considered possible explanations for observed phenomena.

Observations of language-dependent differences in conceptualizations of time (Boroditsky, 2001[1]) and color (Athanasopoulos & Aveledo, 2013) have been interpreted in the context of linguistic relativity. In economics, linguistic relativity was researched empirically by Chen (2013) and Sutter, Angerer, Rützler, and Lergetporer (2015), who attributed differences in intertemporal choices to the used language.

Language-induced differences in dogmatism (Earle 1969), answers to questionnaires (Bond & Yang, 1980; Yang & Bond, 1982; Harzing & Maznevski, 2002), story-telling (Marian & Kaushanskaya, 2004), or cooperative behavior (Akkermans, Harzing, & Van Witteloostuijin, 2010) were interpreted in the context of cultural accommodation or ethnic affirmation.

Theory of foreign language effects has been addressed and refined by studies on loss aversion, ambiguity aversion, and risk aversion (Keysar et al., 2012; Costa et al., 2014a), moral dilemmas (Costa et al., 2014b; Cipolletti et al., 2016; Corey et al., 2017; Hayakawa et al., 2017), cooperation (Urbig et al., 2016), emotional resonance (Dewaele, 2004; Harris, Aycicegi, & Gleason, 2003; Caldwell-Harris, 2009; Harris, 2004; for an overview see Pavlenko, 2005 or Dewaele, 2010), judgment (Geipel, Hadjichristidis, & Surian, 2015; 2016; Hadjichristidis, Geipel, & Savadori, 2015), and memory (Kroll & Tokowicz, 2005; Bartolotti & Marian, 2013; Schrauf & Rubin, 1998; 2000; Shook & Marian; 2012; 2013; Marian & Neisser, 2000; Szmalec, Brysbaert, & Duyck, 2012).

[1]It should be noted that January and Kako (2007) failed to replicate any of Borditsky's (2001) findings that support linguistic relativity, strongly arguing against evidence for linguistic relativity.

2.2.1 Challenges

The landscape of theories is fragmented and lacks internal coherence. Studies that compare groups of people who process tasks in either their mother tongue or a foreign language, often interpret findings solely in the context of one theory. This practice comes with conceptual problems. Linguistic relativity and cultural theories such as cultural accommodation seem to overlap. In addition, language-specific and foreign language effects could coexist and influence behavior simultaneously, potentially adding up or canceling each other out. A considerable share of experimental studies relies on a single foreign language or on several foreign languages that are not paired as a treatment, making it impossible to distinguish between potential effects of linguistic relativity, more general cultural effects, or a foreign language effect (e.g. Keysar et al., 2012; Akkermans et al., 2010; Yang & Bond, 1980; Harzing & Maznevski, 2002; Earle, 1969; Geipel et al. 2016).

On the one hand, studies on possible foreign language effects that fail to rule out language-specific effects are not generalizable to other languages and cultures. On the other hand, studies on linguistic relativity or culture-related effects of language use, which rely on foreign language processing, may misestimate the effects when failing to account for potential general foreign language effects.

Empirical setups must allow disentangling potential effects of language use. Adequate experimental designs, however, require a clear understanding of the relationship between the different theories and effects. In the following, potential overlaps between the theories and other theoretical challenges are identified and discussed.

2.2.1.1 Relationship between Language and Culture

A particular challenge for empirical research on linguistic relativity and cultural effects that may be triggered by language is the endogeneity of language within culture. Culture, in an anthropological definition, can be defined as "*[...] the collective programming of the mind that distinguishes the members of one group or category of people from others.*" (Hofstede, 2011, p. 3). This broad definition allows for different reference frames, potentially allowing for different cultures for groups of all sizes. The most commonly used reference frame for cultural differences are nations, but other reference frames such as geography, social class, or religion could be used to characterize groups of different cultures (Lüsebrink, 2005).

In the anthropological definition of culture stated above, language and culture seem to be closely interrelated. Language itself could be considered an essential part of culture. Taking this view, it would be impossible to have the same culture with different languages as mother tongues. Ultimately, this makes language a subset of culture. One and the same language could still be present in different cultures though, as language is one of many aspects defining culture. Accordingly, linguistic relativity is a sufficient, but not a necessary condition for cultural accommodation. In the context of foreign language use, linguistic relativity is one particular case of cultural accommodation, in which the driving mechanism is the language itself.

Due to this relationship between language and culture, empirical research attempting to disentangle linguistic relativity from cultural accommodation in foreign language contexts seems very challenging. Apart from observing behavioral changes, one would need to identify the specific mechanism and rule out alternative explanations. Chen (2013) and Sutter et al. (2015) explain observed differences in time-preferences across countries with differences in future-time references in languages. They attempt to rule out more general cultural differences as an explanation by controlling for culture, elicited with surveys on values. However, one could criticize that survey answers for values and preferences such as trust or patience are interpreted to define culture, while observed behavior is not. Such a differentiation appears to some degree arbitrary.

In a foreign-language context, I regard cultural accommodation as a suitable aggregate theory that also accounts for linguistic relativity. Cultural accommodation describes effects that can be predicted with linguistic relativity in a more general sense. In particular, cultural accommodation theory allows for a variety of underlying mechanisms, linguistic relativity included.

2.2.1.2 Baseline for "typical" Culture & Ethnic Affirmation

Ethnic affirmation theory implies that people can behave more "typical" for their own culture in a foreign language than in their mother tongue. This raises a question about the baseline of "typical behavior" for a culture.

Applying a national reference frame to culture, Yang and Bond (1980) rely on pre-defined "typical" answers for questionnaires that differ across cultures. In their study, answers from Chinese subjects, who answer the questions in Chinese, are further away from the most "typical" Chinese answers, compared to Chinese subjects who process in English. Applying such a pre-defined baseline for typical behavior can be problematic since it raises the question why people who process in their mother tongue on average should diverge from their typical culture in the first place. One might explain such differences on an individual level, as behavior could be driven by individual and shared cultural values (or with a non-representative sample of participants). Yet, such a view raises another conceptual problem. Individual behavior that differs from "typical" behavior (or a non-representative sample) implies that some other individual (or another non-representative sample) must be on the opposite side of the "typical" answers, assuming that the "typical" answers correspond to the average of the total population. In this case, one could not differentiate between ethnic affirmation and cultural accommodation, as the behavior of individuals (or non-representative samples) could change either way, towards or away from "typical" answers in case of ethnic affirmation.

Any baseline of average typical behavior in a culture should be based on empirical observations and not on pre-defined stereotypes. Accordingly, the baseline of "typical" behavior of a culture must be observable within a sufficiently large and balanced sample of members of that culture processing in their mother tongue.

This conceptual problem in Yang's and Bond's (1980) definition of ethnic affirmation can be addressed with a minor change to the cultural "baseline" implied in their theory. Rather than relying on a pre-defined "typical" behavior, one could rely on actual observed behavior in participant's mother tongue as the baseline for "typical". Ethnic affirmation would still lead to a behavior that is even further away from the "typical" behavior of the foreign culture than the "typical" behavior of one's own culture. Rather than attributing the effect to increased salience of one's own culture when processing in a foreign culture's language, it can be attributed to increased salience of the *difference* between one's own culture and the foreign culture. This slightly modified theory of ethnic affirmation is considered in the rest of this paper, as illustrated in Figure 2.1.

Setting observed behavior as the baseline for "typical" behavior of a culture comes with a methodological challenge. In experimental studies, one detects cultural differences between comparably small subject pools, which might differ from national cultures. When subject pools are not representative of national societies, empirical findings should be interpreted with caution, in particular when performing direct cross-cultural comparisons. Obtaining representative samples of national societies would resolve problems of generalizability in cross-cultural research, but may be rather difficult in practice. In the context of researching effects of language use, it appears highly unlikely that one could find a representative sample that can process an experiment in the desired foreign language, as sufficient knowledge of the foreign language in most cases should be correlated with a higher degree of education. Also, some scholars argue that generalizability can be given even with non-representative subject pools. For example, Gächter, Herrmann, and Thöni (2010) state that the established methodology of cross-cultural experimental research "is to observe a comparable subject pool in different societies." (p. 2653).

Despite potential challenges for generalizability, non-representative subject pools drawn from different national societies are suitable to study the effects of foreign language use. Subject from such pools likely share some characteristics of their respective national cultures. Under this assumption, there seems to be a good chance of detecting potential effects of ethnic affirmation or cultural accommodation in a national sense of culture, even when studying non-representative samples.

2.2.1.3 Asymmetries within Cultural Accommodation and Ethnic Affirmation

The theories of cultural accommodation and ethnic affirmation describe effects of language use that result from cultural differences. One could think of scenarios in which cultural accommodation or ethnic affirmation affects some cultures more than others. Intuitively, a very positive attitude towards a culture could lead to stronger cultural accommodation, as people might be more willing to accommodate to cultures they admire. On the opposite side, a very negative attitude towards a culture could lead to a stronger ethnic affirmation effect, as people might be more prone to distance themselves from the culture they dislike. Attitudes towards cultures are most likely not always symmetric. For example, in the years of the United States—supported the reconstruction of post-WW2 Western Germany, attitudes towards the United States in Germany may have been more positive than attitudes toward Germany in the United States. Apart from attitudes towards cultures, other sources for asymmetries in the effects of cultural accommodation and ethnic affirmation are plausible. For example, knowledge about other cultures may be distributed asymmetrically across countries, or stereotypes could lead to asymmetric effects (Dorrough & Glöckner, 2016).

Accordingly, when comparing two languages and cultures, the effects of cultural accommodation or ethnic affirmation might be in place only uni-directionally, and absent or reversed in the other direction. One should, therefore, differentiate between one-way and two-way cultural accommodation and ethnic affirmation. Within one-way cultural accommodation or ethnic affirmation, one can further differentiate between an effect that is a function of both mother tongue and foreign language, an effect that depends on the mother tongue only, and an effect that depends only on the foreign language. Should an effect depend on both mother tongue and foreign language, one could debate whether attributing such a phenomenon to cultural accommodation or ethnic affirmation would be appropriate. Empirically, such an effect may not be distinguishable from other language-specific effects, that may be caused by mechanisms other than cultural differences.

To my knowledge, these potentially different forms of cultural accommodation or ethnic affirmation have not yet been identified and discussed in the existing literature. Most previous research relies on data of only one foreign language (e.g., Earle, 1969; Akkermans et al., 2010; Harzing & Maznevski, 2002; Yang & Bond, 1980), which makes an identification of possible asymmetries impossible.

2.2.2 Disentangling Potential Effects

Considering the potential overlaps and theoretical challenges of language-induced effects on behavior, one can disentangle cultural accommodation, ethnic affirmation, and foreign language effects. In the following, three different representations help to clarify the topic. Firstly, a graphical representation illustrates directions and differences of the possible effects. Secondly, logical criteria for identifying the individual types of effects are presented. Thirdly, requirements for experimental designs and theoretical limitations are derived from modeling language pairings in a linear equation system.

All representations rely on two languages "*a*" and "*b*". The dependent variable of interest is represented by a combination of two letters that indicate the average behavior of a treatment group. Processing languages are described in lower case letters, while mother tongues are described in upper case letters. For example, "*a_A*" refers to a mother tongue case, in which the processing language "*a*" and the mother tongue "*A*" are identical. Correspondingly, "*a_B*" describes a foreign language case, in which the processing language "*a*" differs from the mother tongue "*B*".

2.2.2.1 Graphical Representation

The different effects of language are illustrated in Figure 2.1 with two languages/cultures "*a*" and "*b*". A single axis represents any behavioral outcome variable. The relative position of foreign language settings to mother tongue settings on the axis illustrates the differences between cultural accommodation and ethnic affirmation. In case of a foreign language effect, there is a common difference "Δ", with an identical, but unspecified direction between mother tongue and foreign language setting, independent of the particular language and mother tongue parings.

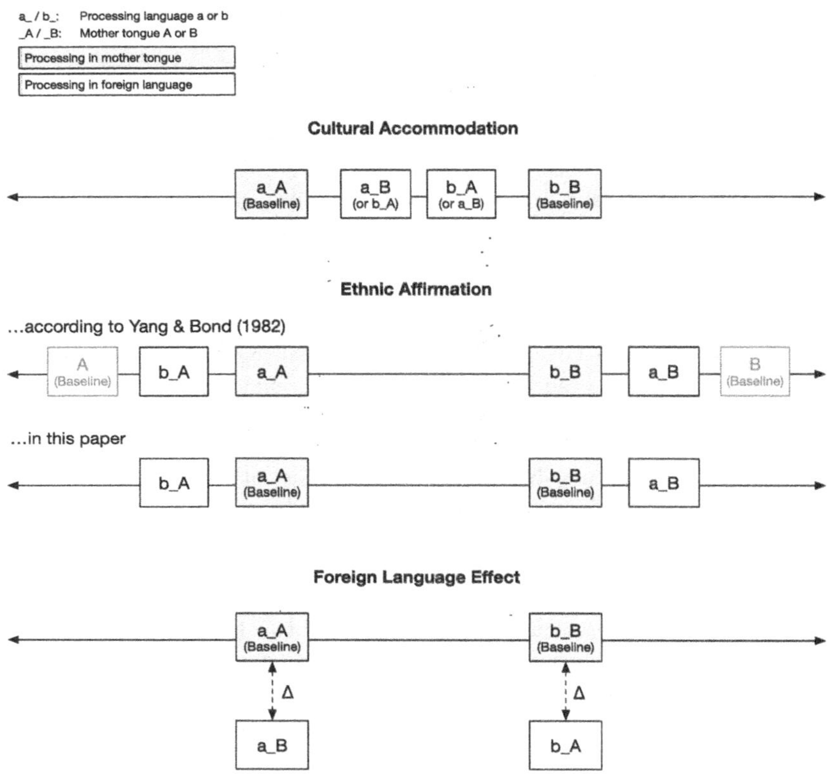

Figure 2.1 Graphical illustration of potential language-induced effects on behavior

2.2.2.2 Logical Statements

Logical statements for identifying potential effects can be derived directly from the graphical representation.

Cultural Differences

$$a\_A \neq b\_B$$

Cultural differences in behavior are a prerequisite for cultural accommodation and ethnic affirmation. They can be observed by comparing the outcomes of two groups of participants with different mother tongues, who process in their mother tongue. This approach corresponds to the previously discussed "baseline of typical behavior". Participants that process in a foreign language (e.g. "a_B") should be excluded from the analysis of cultural differences due to a possible presence of confounding language-induced effects.

Cultural Accommodation
One-sided[2]

$$a\_A \neq b\_B \wedge sgn(a\_B - b\_A) = sgn(a\_A - b\_B)$$

Two-sided

$$a\_A \neq b\_B \wedge sgn(a\_B - b\_B) = -sgn(b\_A - a\_A) = sgn(a\_A - b\_B)$$

Due to potential asymmetries of cultural effects, I distinguish between one-sided and two-sided cultural accommodation. One-sided cultural accommodation applies only to speakers of one of the two mother tongues. Two-sided cultural accommodation applies to native speakers of both languages at the same time.

Ethnic Affirmation
One-sided

$$a\_A \neq b\_B \wedge sgn(a\_B - b\_B) = -sgn(a\_A - b\_B)$$

Two-sided

$$a\_A \neq b\_B \wedge sgn(a\_B - b\_B) = -sgn(b\_A - a\_A) = -sgn(a\_A - b\_B)$$

Ethnic affirmation describes the opposite effect of cultural accommodation and does therefore only differ from cultural accommodation in the sign (i.e., the direction) of the effect.

Foreign Language Effect

$$sgn(a\_B - b\_B) = sgn(b\_A - a\_A) \neq 0$$

The foreign language effect does not require cultural differences and points into the same direction for all cultures.

[2]sgn() refers to the signum function.

2.2.2.3 Requirements for Experimental Research

In order to determine the minimum requirements for factorial designs to clearly distinguish foreign language effects from cultural accommodation or ethnic affirmation, I introduce a simple model. It is based on the assumptions that individuals have a clearly defined mother tongue, and can mentally process inputs in a foreign language setting. The necessary minimum of experimental cells can be derived from corresponding equation systems, comparing unknown variables to the number of equations.

Basic Model

In general, the effect of foreign language use can be modeled as a linear combination of potentially overlapping effects. The outcome variable *"b_A"* for people with mother tongue A that process in language b can be seen as a sum of a baseline-outcome *"a_A"*, a foreign language effect *"FL"* that is constant, and a term *"CA * sgn(b_B-a_A)"* that models cultural accommodation or ethnic affirmation. "CA" is positive in case of cultural accommodation, and a negative in case of ethnic affirmation:

$$b\_A = a\_A + FL + CA{*}sgn(b\_B - a\_A)$$

This simple model illustrates that observing data from only one foreign language treatment (i.e., comparison between one mother tongue and one foreign language) is insufficient to distinguish between a foreign language effect and cultural accommodation or ethnic affirmation. An additional linearly independent equation is required in order to solve for the two unknown variables *"FL"* and *"CA"*. Depending on whether one would like to account for the possibility of partial (i.e., one-way) cultural accommodation/ethnic affirmation or not, several cases can be distinguished:

Case 1: Two-Way Cultural Accommodation or Ethnic Affirmation:

When the foreign language effect, cultural accommodation, and ethnic affirmation apply to speakers of all mother tongues and cultures alike, both unknown variables *"FL"* and *"CA"* are constants. The corresponding model excludes the possibility of one-sided cultural accommodation/ethnic affirmation.

In this case, we can distinguish between a foreign language effect and cultural accommodation/ethnic affirmation by observing all four variations of language use *"a_A"*, *"b_B"*, *"b_A"*, and *"a_B"*. This provides us with a solvable system of two linear equations for the two unknown variables:

$$a\_B = b\_B + FL - CA*sgn(b\_B - a\_A)$$

$$b\_A = a\_A + FL + CA*sgn(b\_B - a\_A)$$

In experimental research, this corresponds to a complete two-by-two factorial design with four cells. Factors are processing language (a, b) and mother tongue (A, B).

Solving for "*CA*" illustrates that "*CA*" is negative in cases of ethnic affirmation, positive in cases of cultural accommodation, and not defined if there are no cultural differences expressed by the term "*(b_B − a_A)*":

$$CA = \frac{b\_B - a\_A + b\_A - a\_B}{2*sgn(b\_B - a\_A)}$$

On the other side, the foreign language effect "*FL*" is independent of cultural differences:

$$FL = \frac{b\_A - a\_A + a\_B - b\_B}{2}$$

Case 2: One-Way Cultural Accommodation or Ethnic Affirmation

When weakening our assumption and allowing for one-sided cultural accommodation or ethnic affirmation, "*CA*" becomes a function of the mother tongue (case 2a), the processing language (case 2b), or possibly even a function of both the mother tongue and the particular processing language (case 2c). The number of unknown variables increases accordingly, requiring more comprehensive data from additional languages to disentangle the effects. Observing data with additional language pairings may help to distinguish between a foreign language effect and the particular influences of cultural accommodation or ethnic affirmation.

Case 2a: Cultural Accommodation or Ethnic Affirmation as a Function of the Mother Tongue

$$a\_B = b\_B + FL - CA\_1*sgn(b\_B - a\_A)$$

$$b\_A = a\_A + FL + CA\_2*sgn(b\_B - a\_A)$$

$$a\_C = c\_C + FL + CA\_3*sgn(a\_A - c\_C)$$

$$b\_C = c\_C + FL + CA\_3 * sgn(b\_B - c\_C)$$

Should the one-sided cultural accommodation only be a function of the mother tongue, we would need to observe at least one additional language paired with both initial languages, in order to obtain four linearly independent equations for the four unknown variables. In experimental research, this corresponds to an incomplete three-by-three factorial design with seven cells.

Case 2b: Cultural Accommodation or Ethnic Affirmation as a Function of the Processing Language

$$a\_B = b\_B + FL - CA\_1 * sgn(b\_B - a\_A)$$

$$b\_A = a\_A + FL + CA\_2 * sgn(b\_B - a\_A)$$

$$a\_C = c\_C + FL + CA\_1 * sgn(a\_A - c\_C)$$

Should the one-sided cultural accommodation only be a function of the processing language, which corresponds to the concept of linguistic relativity, we would need at minimum one additional language paired with one of the initial languages, providing us with three equations for three unknown variables. In experimental research, this corresponds to an incomplete three-by-three factorial design with six cells.

Case 2c: Cultural Accommodation or Ethnic Affirmation as a Function of Both Mother Tongue and Processing Language

Should the one-sided cultural accommodation be a function of both mother tongue and the particular foreign language, it would be impossible to empirically distinguish between a foreign language effect and the particular cultural accommodation effects in experimental settings where the processing language is varied. The number of unknown variables would always exceed the number of equations by at least one. In order to account for the possibility of this case, it seems advisable to elicit additional information on associations between languages and cultures, as well as attitudes towards cultures in experimental settings with varying languages.

2.2.3 Theoretical Conclusion

Comparing and exploring existing theories of possible effects of foreign language reveals possibilities and limitations for empirical research, in particular in experimental contexts.

In experimental research with variations of languages and random subject allocation to mother tongue and foreign language, one can identify and disentangle several potential effects. In particular, one can differentiate between foreign language effects, two-sided cultural accommodation, and two-sided ethnic affirmation. Furthermore, one can identify one-sided cultural accommodation or ethnic affirmation, when the effect is a function only of *either* mother tongue *or* foreign language. If cultural accommodation or ethnic affirmation depended on a particular combination of mother tongue *and* foreign language, one could not disentangle potential cultural effects from foreign language effects using group variations in experimental designs. Mechanisms that potentially drive the effects, such as linguistic relativity, remain hidden. Furthermore, cross-cultural comparisons are limited to the respective subject pools. When subject pools are non-representative samples of cultures, generalizations for cross-cultural research should be made with caution.

2.3 Empirical Exploration

In the following, data from a series of three different experiments are explored in search of language-induced effects on human behavior. The experimental tasks were designed to examine possible foreign language effects on creativity, cheating, and cooperation. Following the logic described in the first part of this paper, this exploratory analysis particularly emphasizes culture-related effects and investigates cultural accommodation and ethnic affirmation. Detailed investigations of foreign language effects on creativity and cooperation are conducted in Chapters 3 and 4.

The experiments were conducted in France, Germany, and the U.S., varying the processing languages between French, German, and English. These three countries show strong systematic differences in common classifications of cultural traits. According to Hofstede's (1991; 2018) classifications of cultural dimensions, France is characterized by a much higher power distance and uncertainty avoidance than Germany and the United States. The latter scores very high on individualism and indulgence, while Germany shows a much higher degree of long-term orientation than the two other countries (see Figure 2.2). Inglehart and Baker (2000) classify cultures in two dimensions. On one axis that depicts traditional vs. secular-rational authorities, Germany is rated as very strongly secular-rational, while the U.S. is in the traditional spectrum. In the survival/self-expression dimension, the U.S. is classified far on the self-expression side, while France is more neutral.

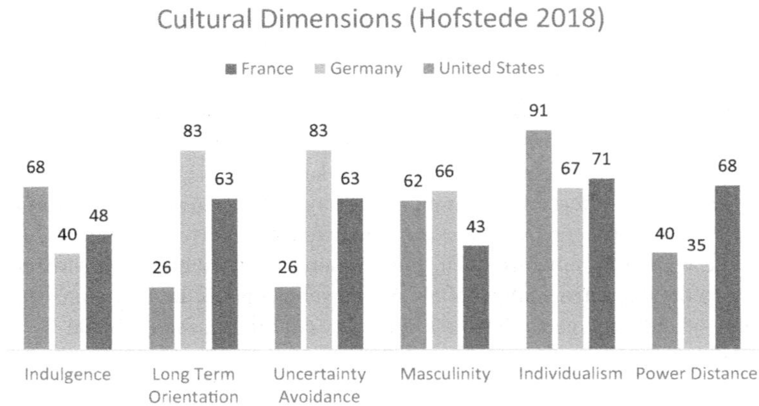

Figure 2.2 Scores of France, Germany, and the U.S. in cultural dimensions according to Hofstede (2018)

Different classifications of France, Germany, and the U.S. indicate that some cultural differences in average behavior are likely to exist between the three countries. Intuitively, Hofstede's (2018) traits of indulgence, masculinity, individualism, and uncertainty avoidance may affect the behavioral domains of this paper, in particularly cheating and cooperation. A study by Niu and Sternberg (2001) on creativity with American and Chinese artists and raters suggests that the domain of creativity is sensitive to cultural differences. Likewise, studying public goods games, Gächter, Hermann, and Thöni (2010) report cultural differences in the domain of cooperation between the U.S. and Germany. Yet, in a cross-cultural meta-study of ultimatum games in 25 countries including France, Germany, and the U.S., Oosterbeek, Sloof, and Van de Kuilen (2004) were not able to attribute findings of cultural differences directly to common cultural traits.

2.3.1 General Setup

In a between-subject design, language students were randomly assigned to conduct tasks in either their mother tongue or a foreign language. Each session was equally split between two processing languages, one being the common mother tongue in the respective country, and the other one being the foreign language of study.

The experiments were conducted with a specifically built mobile laboratory at all locations in order to ensure a comparable experimental environment (see Appendix D). All materials were translated and back-translated by professional translators to ensure comparability (Brislin, 1970). Instructions were given on modified tablet devices that ran the experimental platform oTree (Chen, Schonger, & Wickens, 2016). All experiments were conducted in a single session, varying their order in a latin squares system to control for potential interactions between the tasks. Most tasks were incentivized (100 points = 1 $/€).

The data span seven different mother tongue/processing language combinations, resulting from an incomplete three-by-three factorial design. As shown in the theory section of this paper, incomplete three-by-three factorial designs with seven cells allow to identify effects of one-way cultural accommodation or ethnic affirmation that depend on either mother tongue or foreign processing language.[3]

With language pairings of French-German and English-German, this experimental design allows to distinguish between foreign language effects and cultural accommodation or ethnic affirmation. Subjects' allocation to mother tongue or foreign language is fully randomized, while the allocation to a particular foreign language is only random within the two language pairings. As language-specific effects are analyzed within language pairings, randomization is ensured nevertheless. In terms of sample size, foreign language effects can be analyzed with a larger sample, compared language-specific effects. Cross-cultural comparisons across language pairings are methodologically less rigorous and should be made with caution. Nonetheless, comparable subject pools across language pairings may counterbalance this issue to a certain extent.[4]

---

[3]A complete three-by-three factorial design may prove even more informative, but would increase the operative effort of the data collection significantly, with little methodological advantage.

[4]From an operative point of view, a full random allocation to the treatment language across all language-pairings is a challenge, if not impossible. In the chosen design with three languages, all subjects would need to be trilingual at a high proficiency level.

2.3.2 Priming

All experiments were processed entirely in the respective treatment language, randomly assigned to each participant beforehand. A bilingual experimenter answered potential questions in the respective treatment language. At the beginning of each experimental part, all subjects were given a priming task to increase the salience of the respective processing language. The task was to reproduce a given a short text by writing it out on a sheet of paper. Subsequently, an understanding question was asked to induce reflection on the content of the text. Texts were selected to be easy to understand and neutral with regards to the following experimental tasks.

2.3.3 Subject Pool

All experiments were conducted with 469 language students from seven universities in France, Germany, and the United States. As the focus of this exploration lies on language-specific effects, clearly attributing each participant to one of the three cultures is a critical requirement. Accordingly, participants with multiple mother tongues, or mother tongues different from French, German, or English, were excluded from analysis.[5] The remaining sample consists of 417 participants in seven experimental cells. Table 2.1 summarizes the participant pool, separated by mother tongue and language treatment.

Table 2.1 Subject pool and treatment group characteristics

Mother tongue		*German*	*German*	*German*	*English*	*English*	*French*	*French*
Treatment		*German*	*English*	*French*	*English*	*German*	*French*	*German*
	Total							
Participants	417	103	54	52	63	64	42	39
Age mean	22.85	23.44	23.17	21.71	21.81	22.55	24.50	22.74
Age Std. Dev.	6.04	6.23	3.69	4.25	4.36	6.54	9.58	6.60
Female	65.47%	72.00%	70.37%	80.76%	49.21%	54.68%	69.05%	61.54%
Abroad Experience	63.79%	65.00%	57.40%	63.46%	55.56%	60.94%	73.81%	76.92%

[5]As the experimental design excludes the cells of English processing for participants of French mother tongue and French processing for participants of English mother tongue, an additional participant of French mother tongue and English processing was excluded from analysis.

Language students above a proficiency threshold of B2[6] were chosen to ensure that experimental tasks could be fully understood. Hence, results should not be biased by comprehension errors of the instructions. Furthermore, language students are to some degree comparable subject groups across countries, which is of advantage for cross-cultural comparisons (Gächter et al., 2010). A balance check for age, gender, and abroad experiences in a country associated with the foreign language shows systematic differences between the groups of German mother tongue processing in German, English mother tongue processing in English, and French mother tongue processing in French. These differences are controlled for in the analysis.

2.3.4 Analytical Approach

Language-induced effects on behavior are explored with regression analyses on all outcome variables of the experimental tasks. Rather than focusing on individual dependent variables and their individual interpretation, I compare patterns across the different dependent variables that may support cultural accommodation or ethnic affirmation. An in-depth analysis of foreign language effects on creativity is provided in Chapter 3, and on cooperation in Chapter 4. All regression models in the analysis share the following identical core structure.

$$Y_i = \beta_0 + \beta_1 * mten_i + \beta_2 * mtfr_i + \beta_3 * (en * mtde)_i + \beta_4 * (fr * mtde)_i + \beta_5 * (de * mten)_i + \beta_6 * (de * mtfr)_i + e_i$$

The model describes a dependent variable Y as a function of different mother tongues and processing languages. As the German language is present in all treatment/control pairings, the baseline for all regressions are participants of German mother tongue processing in German. The coefficients *mten* and *mtfr* refer to participants of English and French mother tongues. The interactions *de*mten* and *de*mtfr* describe the differential effect of processing in German for participants of English and French mother tongues, compared to processing in English or French. By including interactions for each combination of foreign language processing and mother tongue without including base variables for the processing languages, the coefficients for interactions directly identify shifts in behavior that are caused by processing in the specific foreign language. For example, *fr*mtde*

[6] B2 categorizes an upper intermediate level in the common European framework of reference for languages.

describes the differential effect of processing in French for participants of German mother tongue, compared to processing in German.

Due to the interactions, *mten* and *mtfr* describe the effect for participants of English or French mother tongues who process in English or French, compared to the baseline of participants of German mother tongue who process in German. Hence, cultural differences between participants of different mother tongues are directly described by the *mten* and *mtfr* coefficients.

The basic model can be extended with additional control variables and interactions to account for systematic differences across the subject pools. Model versions named with the letter "b" include additional independent control variables for age, gender, experience abroad in a country where the treatment language was mainly used to communicate, proficiency, and task orders within the experimental series. Proficiency is based on self-reports on a five-point scale from very low (1) to very high (5). As abroad experience has previously been discussed to potentially influence either creativity (Maddux & Galinsky, 2009; Leung, Maddux, Galinsky, & Chiu, 2008) or effects of language use (Corey et al., 2017; Akkermans et al., 2010), models named with the letter "c" include interactions between abroad experience and a dummy variable *fl* for foreign language processing (*abroad**fl*) to investigate potential interaction effects.

2.3.5 Experiment 1—Creativity

Searching for language-induced effects, I first explore results from a creativity experiment. The experiment measures creative performance with creative products from an incentivized real-effort task.

2.3.5.1 Task

Subjects were asked to illustrate objects of their choice with a given set of material, take a photo of each illustration, and submit the photos on a tablet device. After finishing the illustration task, subjects self-rated their illustrations on creativity, technical goodness (i.e., the technical quality of the illustration), and aesthetic appeal. Subjective ratings by impartial raters on the same aspects were collected in subsequent online sessions to measure creative performance. Impartial raters were blind to the creators' nationality and the language treatment. The raters' creativity scores of each creator's three most highly rated illustrations determined the creator's payoff. Two raters from each of the U.S., Germany, and France were randomly assigned to each illustration. Creators' self-ratings, as well as impartial ratings, were made on a 9-point discrete visual analog scale. Online rating sessions were processed in the common language of each rater's respective country. The illustration task was originally designed by Laske & Schröder (2017), while the applied creativity assessment relies on Amabile's (1996) consensual assessment technique. A detailed description of the experiment is provided in Chapter 3 and instructions are provided in Appendix B.

2.3.5.2 Data

A total of six different dependent variables is analyzed to investigate the role of foreign language processing. Three dependent variables are self-ratings on creativity (*crea self-r.*), technical goodness (*tg self-r.*), and aesthetic appeal (*aa self-r.*), and three dependent variables are impartial ratings on the same aspects (*crea ext. r., tg ext. r., aa ext. r.*). Ratings can range from 1 (low) to 9 (high).

For first overviews, Figure 2.3 and Figure 2.4 show OLS estimates for each combination of mother tongue and processing language with mean and 95% confidence intervals (robust standard errors clustered on participant and impartial rater). The first part of labels refers to the processing language, while the second part refers to the mother tongue. For example, "*en_mtde*" refers to participants of German mother tongue that process in English.

Table 2.2 and Table 2.3 show the main regressions in accordance with the analytical approach described in 3.4. Models 1–3 are OLS regressions for impartial ratings, with robust standard errors clustered on creator and rater. Models 4–6 are OLS regressions for self-ratings with robust standard errors clustered on creator.

2.3.5.3 Results

Results are first discussed for impartial ratings on creativity, technical goodness, and aesthetic appeal, before proceeding with self-ratings on the same aspects.

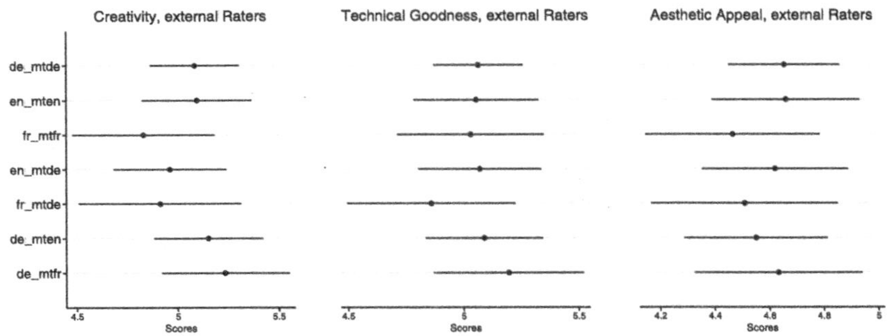

Figure 2.3 OLS estimates of impartial ratings with mean and 95% confidence interval

Table 2.2 OLS regressions on impartial ratings

VARIABLES	(1a) crea ext. r.	(1b) crea ext. r.	(1c) crea ext. r.	(2a) tg ext. r.	(2b) tg ext. r.	(2c) tg ext. r.	(3a) aa ext. r.	(3b) aa ext. r.	(3c) aa ext. r.
mten	0.011	0.016	0.009	-0.009	-0.001	-0.002	0.006	0.029	0.003
	(0.177)	(0.189)	(0.178)	(0.168)	(0.178)	(0.168)	(0.171)	(0.179)	(0.171)
mtfr	-0.254	-0.257	-0.254	-0.033	-0.038	-0.036	-0.189	-0.202	-0.187
	(0.209)	(0.208)	(0.209)	(0.185)	(0.188)	(0.186)	(0.190)	(0.192)	(0.191)
en*mtde	-0.123	-0.098	-0.284	0.006	0.032	-0.068	-0.034	-0.006	-0.149
	(0.158)	(0.151)	(0.193)	(0.142)	(0.137)	(0.169)	(0.149)	(0.141)	(0.173)
fr*mtde	-0.171	-0.176	-0.340	-0.205	-0.212	-0.284	-0.146	-0.157	-0.266
	(0.219)	(0.215)	(0.265)	(0.183)	(0.177)	(0.219)	(0.177)	(0.174)	(0.215)
de*mten	0.057	0.060	-0.114	0.034	0.034	-0.054	-0.111	-0.110	-0.230
	(0.133)	(0.135)	(0.180)	(0.114)	(0.114)	(0.150)	(0.124)	(0.123)	(0.160)
de*mtfr	0.406**	0.375**	0.180	0.164	0.140	0.048	0.168	0.172	0.010
	(0.185)	(0.187)	(0.251)	(0.157)	(0.162)	(0.207)	(0.164)	(0.172)	(0.222)
abroad		0.126	-0.012		0.140	0.053		0.082	-0.029
		(0.114)	(0.132)		(0.093)	(0.103)		(0.096)	(0.115)
abroad*fl			0.277			0.136			0.196
			(0.203)			(0.163)			(0.171)
age		-0.001			-0.009			-0.001	
		(0.012)			(0.010)			(0.010)	
female		0.124			0.125			0.229**	
		(0.107)			(0.090)			(0.094)	
proficiency		-0.048			-0.044			-0.071	
		(0.068)			(0.058)			(0.057)	
order: crea first		-0.210*			-0.116			-0.113	
		(0.114)			(0.093)			(0.096)	
order: crea second		-0.147			-0.127			-0.114	
		(0.125)			(0.104)			(0.107)	
Constant	5.083***	5.269***	5.091***	5.065***	5.357***	5.029***	4.654***	4.824***	4.673***
	(0.113)	(0.483)	(0.142)	(0.099)	(0.428)	(0.115)	(0.104)	(0.413)	(0.126)
Observations	13,380	13,380	13,380	13,380	13,380	13,380	13,380	13,380	13,380
R-squared	0.002	0.005	0.004	0.001	0.004	0.002	0.001	0.004	0.001

OLS regressions. Robust standard errors clustering for impartial raters and creators in parentheses
*** $p<0.01$, ** $p<0.05$, * $p<0.1$

Impartial Ratings (Models 1–3)

For impartial ratings on creativity (models 1a-c), no cultural difference is observable between German and English. Participants of French mother tongue, who process in French, have lower ratings, but without statistical significance (*mtfr*). Models 1a and 1b show a significantly positive effect of processing in German for subjects of French mother tongue (*de*mtfr*). This effect is particularly strong for participants with abroad experience (model 1c: Wald test *abroad*fl* + *de*mtfr*, p = 0.015). For participants of German mother tongue who process in French, the coefficient *fr*mtde* is negative, but not significant (model 1a). The patterns seem robust for controls (model 1b). The strongly positive coefficient for the interaction of abroad experience and foreign language processing (*abroad*fl* in model 1c) indicates a potential moderating role of abroad experience but is statistically not significant. While the overall directions of French/German coefficients would be in line with cultural accommodation, they are not significant. Furthermore, the different signs of coefficients for foreign language processing speak against a foreign language effect.

Models 2a-c do not show cultural differences for impartial ratings on technical goodness (*mten, mtfr*). Coefficients for foreign language processing are not significant and point in different directions, which speaks against a foreign language effect. Results are robust for controls (model 2b). Theories of cultural accommodation and ethnic affirmation predict no effect of foreign language processing in the absence of cultural differences. Effect sizes of foreign language coefficients are not zero, but given the lack of significance, this may be a coincidence.

Models 3a-c do not reveal statistically significant cultural differences for the aesthetic appeal of the illustrations. Yet, the coefficient for *mtfr* is negative while *mten* is almost zero. Positive coefficients for *de*mtfr* in models 3a and a negative coefficient for *fr*mtde* are in line with cultural accommodation, but a lack of robustness to controls and statistical significance does not allow for meaningful conclusions. Coefficients for foreign language processing are not significant and point in different directions, which speaks against a foreign language effect. Also, female participants have obtained significantly higher scores on aesthetic appeal than their male counterparts.

Lacking clear cultural differences, models 1–3 should be well-suited to detect potential general foreign language effects. No such effects can be observed. While data of these dependent variables is not ideal for detecting cultural accommodation or ethnic affirmation, the directions of the coefficients seem to be more in line with cultural accommodation than with ethnic affirmation.

Self-Ratings (Models 4–6)

All models from 4a) to 6b) show significant cultural difference between French and German. According to the theories of cultural accommodation and ethnic affirmation, these cultural differences should be visible in the interactions

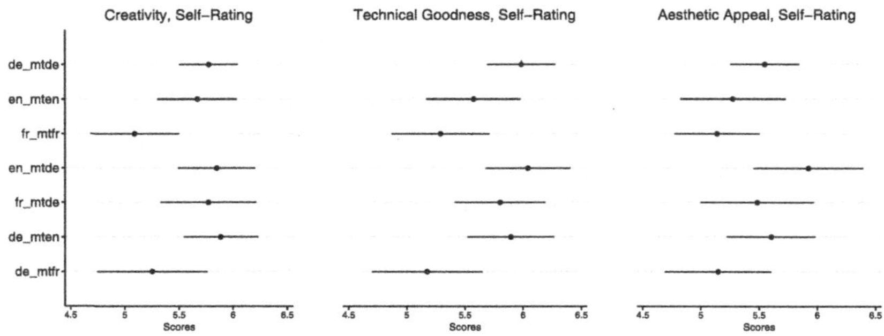

Figure 2.4 OLS estimates of self-ratings with mean and 95% confidence interval

Table 2.3 OLS regressions on self-ratings

VARIABLES	(4a) crea self-r.	(4b) crea self-r.	(4c) crea self-r.	(5a) tg self-r.	(5b) tg self-r.	(5c) tg self-r.	(6a) aa self-r.	(6b) aa self-r.	(6c) aa self-r.
mten	-0.106	-0.041	-0.030	-0.410	-0.318	-0.333	-0.274	-0.208	-0.211
	(0.233)	(0.235)	(0.219)	(0.253)	(0.261)	(0.244)	(0.271)	(0.271)	(0.263)
mtfr	-0.684***	-0.683***	-0.723***	-0.695**	-0.678**	-0.734***	-0.410*	-0.425*	-0.443*
	(0.249)	(0.254)	(0.255)	(0.269)	(0.271)	(0.270)	(0.244)	(0.247)	(0.249)
en*mtde	0.072	0.063	0.654**	0.057	0.023	0.667**	0.373	0.360	0.863***
	(0.239)	(0.235)	(0.294)	(0.249)	(0.243)	(0.310)	(0.285)	(0.285)	(0.328)
fr*mtde	-0.004	0.012	0.586*	-0.183	-0.165	0.437	-0.066	-0.037	0.431
	(0.266)	(0.264)	(0.329)	(0.252)	(0.248)	(0.326)	(0.297)	(0.291)	(0.388)
de*mten	0.219	0.194	0.737**	0.319	0.290	0.867**	0.329	0.295	0.766**
	(0.255)	(0.250)	(0.332)	(0.278)	(0.270)	(0.342)	(0.294)	(0.286)	(0.379)
de*mtfr	0.163	0.162	0.854**	-0.114	-0.117	0.615	0.008	0.044	0.590
	(0.324)	(0.331)	(0.428)	(0.322)	(0.330)	(0.428)	(0.295)	(0.300)	(0.427)
abroad		0.120	0.621***		0.040	0.631***		0.103	0.523**
		(0.168)	(0.201)		(0.177)	(0.220)		(0.186)	(0.225)
abroad*fl			-0.911***			-0.959***			-0.767**
			(0.308)			(0.318)			(0.348)
age		0.017			0.012			0.026	
		(0.016)			(0.014)			(0.017)	
female		-0.076			-0.146			-0.125	
		(0.162)			(0.166)			(0.182)	
proficiency		0.111			0.217**			0.095	
		(0.088)			(0.101)			(0.098)	
order: crea first		0.026			0.121			0.200	
		(0.167)			(0.175)			(0.184)	
order: crea second		0.181			0.062			0.332	
		(0.192)			(0.201)			(0.211)	
Constant	5.774***	4.819***	5.360***	5.985***	4.795***	5.564***	5.550***	4.398***	5.201***
	(0.143)	(0.603)	(0.180)	(0.153)	(0.633)	(0.201)	(0.151)	(0.653)	(0.195)
Observations	2,230	2,230	2,230	2,230	2,230	2,230	2,230	2,230	2,230
R-squared	0.012	0.018	0.023	0.019	0.032	0.033	0.012	0.021	0.020

OLS regressions. Robust standard errors clustering for impartial raters and creators in parentheses

*** $p<0.01$, ** $p<0.05$, * $p<0.1$

*de*mtfr* and *fr*mtde*. However, the pattern of these two interactions is somewhat inconsistent across models 4–6. This speaks against both theories of cultural accommodation and ethnic affirmation.

The self-rating data indicates that a foreign language effect may be in place. Overall, coefficients for foreign language processing differ substantially across the particular combinations of foreign language and mother tongue. However, interacting foreign language processing with abroad experience reveals a strong moderation effect of having lived abroad (*abroad*fl* in models 4c, 5c, & 6c).

Participants *without* abroad experience show overall strongly positive and to a large degree significant coefficients for foreign-language processing. Jointly, the foreign language processing coefficients are strongly significant (Wald tests *en*mtde* + *fr*mtde* + *de*mten* + *de*mtfr*, model 4c: $p = 0.007$; model 5c: $p = 0.016$; model 6c: $p = 0.023$), revealing a foreign language effect for participants without abroad experience. People without abroad experience tend to rate their illustrations higher when they use a foreign language.

For participants *with* abroad experience, no foreign language effect can be observed. The strongly negative coefficients for *fl*abroad* offset the positive coefficients for foreign language processing in models 4c, 5c, and 6c.

Among the control variables, proficiency has a positive effect on self-ratings of technical goodness (*proficiency* in model 5b). Coefficients for proficiency are also positive for the other self-ratings, but not significant. Intuitively, a higher proficiency may increase self-confidence, which may be reflected in higher self-ratings.

2.3.6 Experiment 2—Cheating

The second experiment explored in this paper is an incentivized test for average cheating tendencies across treatment and control groups, initially designed by Fischbacher and Föllmi-Heusi (2013).

2.3.6.1 Task

Subjects were given a regular six-sided die and an overview of corresponding payments for each outcome of the die roll (Table 2.4). They were then asked to roll the die privately as many times as they wanted and report the result of their first roll to determine the payment. Testing dividers around the subjects shielded the die from observers, ensuring that subjects were able to report any result without the possibility of verification by a third person. Accordingly, it was impossible to detect individual lies, and any false reports would have no consequences for subjects except for different payments. Cheating behavior is observed by comparing the distributions of reported die rolls across groups.

Table 2.4 Payment table. 100 points correspond to 1 €/$

Result die roll	1	2	3	4	5	6
Payment [points]	100	200	300	400	500	0

2.3.6.2 Data

The dependent variable is each participant's reported payoff. Results are first analyzed on an aggregate level, followed by a more detailed analysis of each payoff category. The regression analyses rely on the approach introduced in paragraph 3.4.

2.3.6.3 Results

In the absence of cheating, the distribution of die rolls should be uniform with a probability of 100%/6 = 16.7% for each outcome. Results are presented starting with descriptive histograms before regressions are conducted on an aggregate level (Tobit), and in detail on each outcome (Probit).

Figure 2.5 provides a graphical overview of the reported results by each subgroup of a particular mother tongue and processing language combination. Table 2.5 shows Tobit regressions with the payoff as the dependent variable, and independent variables analogous to paragraph 3.4.

On an aggregate level, cultural differences are absent or rather weak. While participants of German mother tongue who processed in German appear to have higher average payoffs than participants of English mother tongue who processed in English, differences are neither statistically significant in means (*mten* in models 7a-b), nor in distribution (Kolmogorov-Smirnov test $p = 0.40$; Wilcoxon Rank-Sum test $p = 0.149$). Furthermore, cultural differences between French and German are clearly insignificant on either of the tests (*mtfr* in models 7a-b; Kolmogorov-Smirnov test $p = 0.99$; Wilcoxon Rank-Sum test $p = 0.84$).

Different directions of coefficients for foreign language interactions in models 7a-b speak against a general foreign language effect on cheating. Patterns are robust for controls.

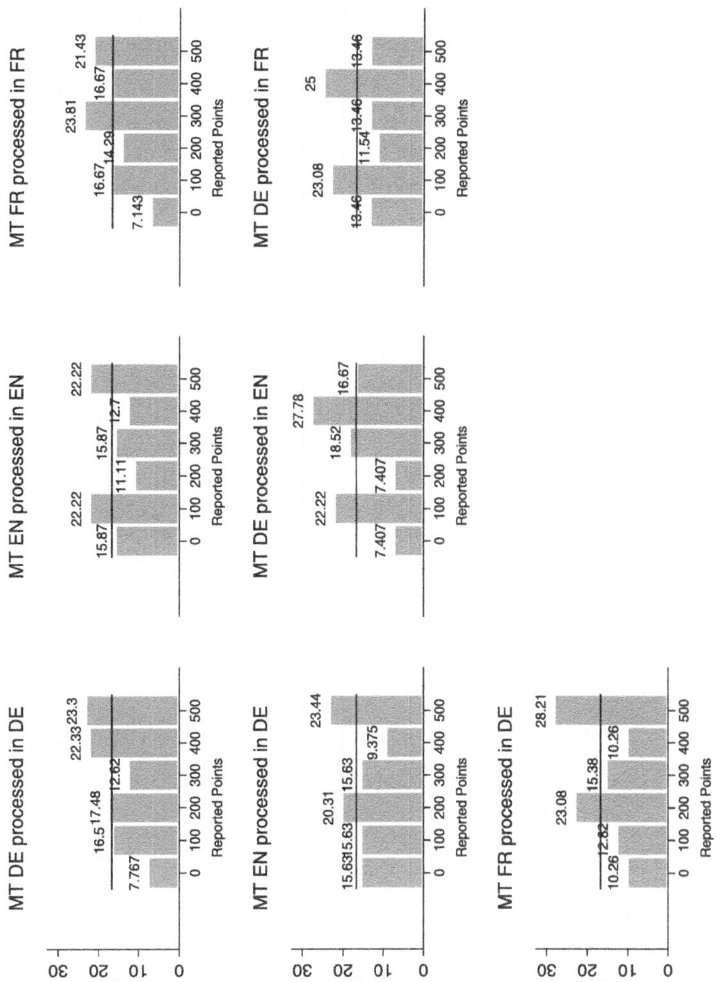

Figure 2.5 Overview of payoff distributions

The strongly negative, yet statistically insignificant interaction between abroad experience and foreign language processing indicates a possible moderating effect of abroad experience (*abroad*fl* in model 7c, p = 0.343). Differentiating between participants with and without abroad experience reveals a marginally significant negative effect on cheating for participants of German mother tongue with abroad

Table 2.5 Tobit regressions on payoffs

VARIABLES	(7a) payoff	(7b) payoff	(7c) payoff
mten	-55.719	-39.011	-53.391
	(39.300)	(40.351)	(39.378)
mtfr	-6.953	-6.262	-9.447
	(44.755)	(44.579)	(44.835)
en*mtde	-17.619	-12.788	11.719
	(40.927)	(40.646)	(51.056)
fr*mtde	-64.291	-64.109	-33.674
	(41.498)	(41.286)	(52.457)
de*mten	6.114	3.991	34.006
	(43.694)	(43.370)	(52.803)
de*mtfr	2.579	8.968	38.574
	(54.628)	(54.363)	(66.666)
abroad		11.210	28.569
		(26.565)	(35.604)
abroad*fl			-47.808
			(50.384)
age		1.246	
		(2.140)	
female		44.205*	
		(25.834)	
proficiency		10.099	
		(13.932)	
order: task second		4.386	
		(29.688)	
order: task first		63.135*	
		(32.219)	
Constant	318.347***	184.107**	299.928***
	(24.184)	(90.604)	(33.275)
Observations	417	417	417

Tobit regression, ll(0), ul(500). Standard errors in parentheses
*** p<0.01, ** p<0.05, * p<0.1

experience who processed in French (model 7c, Wald test *abroad*fl* + *fr*mtde*, p = 0.073). Regarding the control variables, females and participants who processed the task first, compared to the other tasks, have cheated more on a marginal level of significance.

In the following, more detailed insights are drawn from investigating each of the possible outputs of the die roll. It should be noted that the frequencies of payoff steps are not independent of each other, as they must add up to 100% by design (Table 2.6).

Table 2.6 Payoff distributions by treatment group

Language		Payments [points]						
Processed in	**Mother Tongue**	**0**	**100**	**200**	**300**	**400**	**500**	**n**
German	German	7.76**	16.5	17.48	12.62	22.33	23.3*	103
English	English	15.87	22.22	11.11	15.87	12.7	22.22	63
French	French	7.14	16.67	14.29	23.81	16.67	21.43	42
English	German	7.41*	22.22	7.41*	18.52	27.78**	16.67	54
French	German	13.46	23.08	11.54	13.46	25	13.46	52
German	English	15.63	15.63	20.31	15.62	9.38	23.44	64
German	French	10.26	12.82	23.08	15.38	10.26	28.21*	39

Percentage of reported payoffs by treatment. Stars display the significance of two-sided binomial tests that the observed frequency is different from 100%/6 (16.7%). * =10%-level ** =5%-level *** =1%-level

Some cultural differences appear to exist when looking at payoffs of 0 points. Two-sided binomial tests on whether the observed frequencies of reported payoffs are significantly different from 16.7% reveal likely cheating behavior for participants of German mother tongue processing in German or English. The payoff distributions for participants of English mother tongue processing in English or German speak against strong cheating behavior, as most frequencies are close to 16.7%. In particular, frequencies of participants with 0 payoffs, which Fischbacher and Föllmi-Heusi (2013) interpret as completely honest, are close to 16.7% for participants of English mother tongue, regardless of the processing language. Payoff distributions for participants of French mother tongue resemble those of German mother tongue participants but lack statistical significance, likely due to a smaller n.

Regression analysis of frequencies of each particular payoff does not reveal any apparent effects of language. Table 2.7 contains results of Probit regressions for each of the payoffs, with independent variables analogous to model 1. In these regressions, cultural differences are not statistically significant, despite some high effect sizes for *mten* in models 8 and 12. Considering these effect sizes, coefficients of negligible size for *en*mtde* and *de*mten* for payoff_0 (model 8) and their directions for payoff_400 (model 12) speak against the theory of cultural accommodation and ethnic affirmation.

Across models 8–13, the influence of processing in foreign languages appears to be rather small. Most coefficients for interactions that include a foreign language dummy are statistically insignificant and do not share common directions, speaking against a general foreign language effect. Size and direction of the coefficients *fr*mtde* for low payoffs (models 8–9) indicate that processing in French may decrease cheating for participants of German mother tongue. While the coefficient is not statistically significant, it is in line with the previously observed negative effect of French processing for participants of German mother tongue, that is contingent on abroad experience.

Table 2.7 Probit regressions on payoffs

VARIABLES	(8) payoff_0	(9) payoff_100	(10) payoff_200	(11) payoff_300	(12) payoff_400	(13) payoff_500
mten	0.421	0.209	-0.285	0.145	-0.380	-0.036
	(0.263)	(0.230)	(0.255)	(0.247)	(0.244)	(0.223)
mtfr	-0.044	0.006	-0.132	0.432	-0.206	-0.063
	(0.344)	(0.274)	(0.280)	(0.265)	(0.268)	(0.257)
en*mtde	-0.025	0.209	-0.511*	0.249	0.172	-0.238
	(0.313)	(0.241)	(0.293)	(0.253)	(0.228)	(0.245)
fr*mtde	0.316	0.238	-0.263	0.040	0.087	-0.376
	(0.284)	(0.242)	(0.270)	(0.270)	(0.234)	(0.258)
de*mten	-0.010	-0.245	0.390	-0.010	-0.177	0.040
	(0.269)	(0.259)	(0.275)	(0.269)	(0.297)	(0.247)
de*mtfr	0.198	-0.167	0.331	-0.308	-0.300	0.215
	(0.399)	(0.344)	(0.327)	(0.324)	(0.357)	(0.305)
Constant	-1.421***	-0.974***	-0.936***	-1.144***	-0.761***	-0.729***
	(0.182)	(0.148)	(0.145)	(0.158)	(0.138)	(0.136)
Observations	417	417	417	417	417	417

PROBIT Regressions. Robust standard errors in parentheses
*** $p<0.01$, ** $p<0.05$, * $p<0.1$

In conclusion, results of this experiment weakly speak against the theories of cultural accommodation and ethnic affirmation. Furthermore, a general foreign language effect on cheating cannot be observed. Contingent on abroad experience, there appears to be a negative language-specific effect on cheating for participants of German mother tongue who process in French. Sporadic differences across other treatment groups support contradicting theories and are likely a product of chance. However, given the rather weak cultural differences, the informative value of this experiment for cultural accommodation or ethnic affirmation is small.

2.3.7 Experiment 3—Cooperation

The third experiment is a social dilemma designed to investigate cooperative behavior.

2.3.7.1 Task

Subjects were given an anonymous one-shot continuous prisoner's dilemma without communication (Wahl & Nowak, 1999; Dorrough & Glöckner, 2006). Two randomly matched subjects were given identical tasks in which they had to make an identical decision without knowing their partner's decision. Each subject was presented with an initial endowment of 300 points, which she could either transfer in parts (multiples of 30 points) or entirely to her unknown partner, or keep for herself. Transferred points are lost for the transferring player, and doubled for the receiving player. Accordingly, the possible payment for each player lies between 0 and 900 points, depending on both subject's decisions. The Nash equilibrium predicts no transfer of points, resulting in a payment of 300 points for each subject, while the social optimum would be a full transfer of all points, resulting in a payment of 600 points for each subject.

After making their transfer decision, each participant was asked for their expectation regarding the other player's transfer.

2.3.7.2 Data and Results

The dependent variables investigated for language-induced effects on behavior are the outgoing transfer (*transfer*) and expected incoming transfer from the other player (*expected transfer*). Analogous to experiment 1, the analysis consists of a graphical representation of OLS estimates for each group of the elicited language combinations (Figure 2.6), and main regressions in accordance with the approach described in paragraph 3.4 (Table 2.8).

Results do not indicate significant cultural differences between participant groups processing in their mother tongues (*mten, mtfr*).

For participants of German mother tongue, processing in French appears to have a strongly positive impact on the transfer of points (*fr*mtde* in models 14a-b). This language-specific effect is present despite the lack of cultural differences between French and German mother tongue participants. Accordingly, the effect can neither be attributed to cultural accommodation, nor to ethnic affirmation.

Furthermore, no general foreign language effect on cooperation can be observed, as there is no common pattern for effects of foreign language processing (models 14a-b). Coefficients for German processing for participants of French (*de*mtfr*) or English (*de*mten*) mother tongues are negligible in size and not

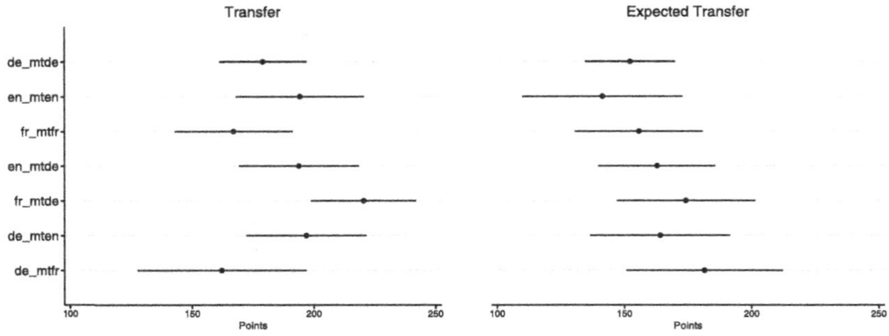

Figure 2.6 OLS estimates of transfers and expected transfers with mean and 95% confidence interval

Table 2.8 OLS regressions on transfers and expected transfers

VARIABLES	(14a) transfer	(14b) transfer	(14c) transfer	(15a) exp. transfer	(15b) exp. transfer	(15c) exp. transfer
mten	15.160	18.565	14.589	-10.902	-6.096	-12.299
	(16.168)	(15.964)	(16.216)	(18.396)	(18.385)	(18.435)
mtfr	-11.983	-12.352	-11.457	3.384	4.701	4.674
	(15.367)	(16.035)	(15.453)	(15.650)	(16.310)	(15.665)
en*mtde	14.763	16.626	-4.028	10.448	12.167	-8.689
	(15.498)	(15.412)	(19.725)	(14.798)	(14.495)	(20.275)
fr*mtde	41.258***	46.402***	20.898	21.901	25.279	1.756
	(14.302)	(14.671)	(19.239)	(16.513)	(17.136)	(21.080)
de*mten	2.589	2.782	-16.547	22.634	23.191	4.307
	(18.285)	(17.880)	(21.681)	(21.270)	(20.805)	(23.705)
de*mtfr	-4.835	-3.718	-29.212	25.824	27.165	2.148
	(21.515)	(21.648)	(26.015)	(20.216)	(20.481)	(25.161)
abroad		6.304	-6.007		-1.853	-14.721
		(10.393)	(13.689)		(10.883)	(14.890)
abroad*fl			31.933			31.375
			(19.660)			(20.730)
age		1.625**			1.349*	
		(0.697)			(0.796)	
female		-10.735			3.289	
		(10.019)			(10.667)	
proficiency		6.966			7.030	
		(5.352)			(5.512)	
order: prisoner's d. third		-10.964			-18.306	
		(11.439)			(12.350)	
order: prisoner's d. first		15.635			14.325	
		(12.257)			(13.421)	
Constant	179.126***	113.310***	183.034***	152.330***	91.077**	161.906***
	(9.134)	(32.954)	(12.427)	(9.041)	(36.759)	(13.077)
Observations	417	417	417	417	417	417
R-squared	0.030	0.061	0.039	0.014	0.039	0.019

OLS regressions. Robust standard errors in parentheses
*** p<0.01, ** p<0.05, * p<0.1

significant (models 14a-b). The coefficient for processing in English for participants of German mother tongue (*en*mtde*) is positive, but not significant (models 14a-b).

However, there is some support for a positive foreign language effect on expected transfers: In models 15a-b, interactions between mother tongues and foreign languages share a positive direction and are jointly significant (Wald test *en*mtde + fr*mtde + de*mten + de*mtfr*; model 15a: $p = 0.039$; model 15b: $p = 0.025$).

Abroad experience by itself does not seem to affect cooperation or expected cooperation (*abroad* in models 14a-b, 15a-b), but the strongly positive coefficients of the interaction between abroad experience and foreign language processing (*abroad*fl*, $p = 0.105$ in model 14c; $p = 0.131$ in model 15c) hint towards a possible moderating effect.

Overall, data of experiment 3 is not in line with cultural accommodation and ethnic affirmation. While no foreign language effect can be observed on cooperation, the data support a positive foreign language effect on expected cooperation from the other player. In addition, the analysis reveals a language-specific positive effect of French processing for participants of German mother tongue on transfers, which cannot be explained by any of the theories discussed in this paper.

2.3.8 Empirical Interpretation

Combining the explorative results of the three experiments leads to an overall mixed picture. The following paragraphs summarize findings on cultural differences, cultural accommodation and ethnic affirmation, other language-specific effects, and foreign language effects.

Cultural Differences

Of the nine different dependent variables explored in our analysis, only four reveal cultural differences as defined in this paper. No statistically significant cultural differences are observed for the prisoner's dilemma and for impartial ratings on creativity, technical goodness, and aesthetic appeal in experiment one. Self-ratings on the same aspects reveal some definite cultural differences, while the die roll experiment reveals some weak cultural differences. Considering the presumed overall strong cultural differences between France, Germany, and the U.S., as reported by Hofstede (2018) and Inglehart & Baker (2000), these findings are surprising. Moreover, they stand in contrast to previous research on cultural differences in prisoner's dilemmas and the closely related public goods game. Wong and Hong (2005) have observed effects of cultural priming in prisoner's dilemmas with American-Chinese biculturals. Gächter et al. (2010) report cultural differences in cooperation, based on public goods games in 15 countries, including the U.S. (Boston) and Germany (Bonn). Dorrough and Glöckner (2016) report cultural differences and influences of cultural stereotypes in continuous prisoner's dilemmas in six countries.

Cultural Accommodation & Ethnic Affirmation
Due to limited cultural differences, possibilities of observing effects of cultural accommodation or ethnic affirmation are limited. The theories predict language-induced effects only in areas with cultural differences. In such areas, for example, the self-ratings in the first experiment, neither theory is supported by the overall observed patterns. Occasional effects that are in line with either cultural accommodation or ethnic affirmation are reversed in other areas. Other language-specific effects and pure chance seems to be the most convincing explanation for these phenomena.

Other Language-Specific Effects
The explorative analysis reveals a few specific effects of single combinations of mother tongue and foreign language, that cannot be attributed to the discussed theories. Given the high number of variables, such findings may be a coincidence. Attempting to replicate effects of processing in French for participants of German mother tongue on expected cooperation, as well as creativity effects of processing in German for participants of French mother tongue seems therefore advisable.

Foreign Language Effects
A general foreign language effect cannot be observed for impartial ratings of creativity, technical goodness, or aesthetic appeal in experiment 1, cheating in experiment 2, or cooperation in experiment 3.

However, I do observe a foreign language effect on self-ratings of creativity, technical goodness, and aesthetic appeal, that is moderated by abroad experience: While self-ratings from participants without abroad experience in a country of the foreign treatment language seem to be affected by a positive foreign language effect, this effect is absent for participants with abroad experience.

Another foreign language effect may affect expected cooperation in the prisoner's dilemma game. Data indicates that participants who process in a foreign language, expect the other player to cooperate more, compared to participants who process in their mother tongue. Despite a lack of statistical significance, data from experiment 3 also hints towards a positive moderating effect of abroad experience on both cooperation and expected cooperation. For future empirical research on language-induced effects, it is therefore advisable to account for possible moderation of abroad experiences. A detailed analysis of foreign language effects on cooperation is provided in Chapter 4.

2.4 Conclusion and Limitations

This paper consists of a theoretical and an explorative empirical part.

In the theoretical part, possible effects of foreign language use are discussed and compared. Three new theoretical arguments are made. First, linguistic relativity should be treated as a special case of cultural accommodation when applied in a foreign language use context. Second, the baseline of "typical" behavior for a certain culture should be derived directly from observed behavior. Exogenous baselines of "typical" behavior, as used in some previous research, would make it impossible to distinguish cultural accommodation from ethnical affirmation empirically. Third, possible asymmetries between cultures in cultural accommodation may exist and encumber empirical research. In case of one-sided cultural accommodation as a function of both mother tongue and foreign language, such effects may be inseparable from other language-specific effects in experimental settings that vary the processing language.

Differences between the theories of foreign language effects, cultural accommodation, and ethnic affirmations are illustrated graphically and with logical relations. Possibilities and limitations for empirical research on possible effects are then derived from a newly introduced model of language-related effects.

In the explorative empirical part of this paper, data from a series of three experiments in three countries is investigated to identify possible effects of foreign language use. A special focus lies on the theories of cultural accommodation and ethnic affirmation. The experiments cover different domains of human behavior, eliciting nine dependent variables around creative performance, aesthetics, self-ratings, cheating, and cooperation. Overall, results show an unexpectedly low level of cultural differences, which are a prerequisite for potential effects of cultural accommodation or ethnic affirmation. Data from self-rating tasks on creativity, technical goodness, and aesthetics shows clear cultural differences and contradict theories of cultural accommodation and ethnic affirmation for these domains. General foreign language effects are rare but may affect the expected cooperative behavior of others, and self-ratings for participants without abroad experience.

As with any empirical study, the explorative analysis of experiments in different mother tongues and processing languages conducted in this paper is subject to limitations.

The empirical data is limited to the *domains* of creativity, aesthetics, cheating, and cooperation. It is possible that foreign language processing affects other domains of human behavior differently.

The *assignment* to mother tongue or foreign language is fully randomized, while the assignment to a specific processing language is only random within subject pools of language pairings. Accordingly, inferences on foreign language effects can be drawn from larger group sizes than inferences on language-specific effects. However, my analysis is of language-specific effects relies on comparisons within language pairings, in which randomization to the two specific languages is given.

The overall experimental design is well-suited to analyze possible effects of foreign language use, yet the particular tasks and subject pools may not be ideal for determining cultural differences. *Tasks* were initially chosen to research a possible foreign language effect and not based on possible interactions with culture. It would be interesting to analyze experimental tasks specifically designed to test cultural differences or to use tasks that have revealed strong cultural differences across France, Germany, and the U.S. in previous studies. For example, Oosterbeek, Sloop, and Van De Kuilen (2003) report cultural differences between countries in a comparison of ultimatum game experiments.

Another possible explanation for a lack of cultural differences could be the similarity of *subjects pools* across countries. Language students in the age group of 20–30 years may share a common sub-culture that dominates their national culture.

For most countries in the world, subject pools that are able to process tasks in a foreign language are per se not a representative sample of the country's society. Foreign language proficiency itself is an indicator of higher education or an above-average exposure to corresponding foreign cultures. Accordingly, the generalizability of findings from this study's subjects can be debated. However, testing comparable subject pools across different countries is a straight-forward and proven methodology to identify cultural differences (Gächter et al., 2010). In the foreign-language context of this paper, comparable subject pools across different countries appear to be the best workable option. In order to improve the generalizability of findings to national cultures, one could test additional subject pools from France, Germany, and the U.S., comprised of different educational backgrounds and age groups.

Data in the empirical part of this paper is regionally limited to "Western" societies. While the subject pools originate from six different cities, the experiments target only a small excerpt of the world. Findings may therefore not be generalizable to other countries or regions. In particular, cultural differences may be more present or stronger when comparing western countries to countries in Africa or Asia.

Another limitation to discuss is the *priming*. In this study, cognitive processing cannot be observed. Hence, one can only trust that the priming, consisting of text reproduction, questions, and instructions in the foreign language, does indeed trigger mental processing in a foreign language. Participants may simply translate the tasks to their mother tongue and back-translate answers to the foreign language. However, in many ways, the tasks resemble "real-life" situations of using a foreign language outside of the laboratory. It seems plausible that participants in the treatment group engage at least to some degree in cognitive processing in the foreign language, but there is no certainty. For future studies in the field, it would be interesting to elicit additional physiological indicators of differences in cognitive processing, such as event-related brain potentials (ERP). More insights from neuroscientific research, as provided by Wu and Thierry (2012a; 2012b), could help to understand the cognitive mechanisms behind foreign language processing better.

Despite its limitations, this paper contributes to research by clearly disentangling several potential effects of foreign language. Based on comparisons of theories and discussions of overlaps, it derives possibilities and requirements to research such effects in experimental designs. The additional explorative analysis of experimental data from three experiments extends our knowledge about the relevance of cultural accommodation, ethnic affirmation, and foreign language effects to new domains.

Perhaps more importantly, it demonstrates conceptual challenges that are problematic in previous research on language-induced effects. Given that this paper identifies no support for the main theories, replication studies on previous findings in a methodologically more rigorous setup seem to be a good way to move forward. This paper's theoretical framework and its experimental design could be of help to improve our understanding of the role of language in human behavior.

3 Foreign Language Effects on Creativity

3.1 Introduction

A large part of the world's population regularly interacts and works in foreign languages. The international business world relies heavily on English as a lingua franca (Neeley, 2012). Our institutions are shaped by intergovernmental organizations whose employees conduct large parts of their work in foreign language settings[1]. The five most common languages on the internet account for about 75% of the world's websites (W3Techs, 2018). Foreign language use is ubiquitous. Yet, we know surprisingly little about potential effects of foreign language use on human behavior.

Characteristics of language may influence thought and behavior, as stated by the concept of linguistic relativity (Kay and Kempton 1984). In addition, recent studies report that using a foreign language could affect behavior per se, regardless of the specific language. Researchers have identified foreign language effects on decision biases (e.g., Keysar, Hayakawa, & An, 2012; Costa et al., 2014a) and moral choices (Corey et al., 2017; Hayakawa et al., 2017). Potential foreign language effects on many other aspects of human behavior have not yet been researched. Thus, scope and relevance of foreign language effects are mostly unknown.

This paper investigates the effects of foreign language use on creativity. Creativity is a crucial factor for innovation, and the ability to develop something novel and useful is a key asset in many types of work. Some fields of work that heavily rely on creativity (e.g., science; research & development in multinational corporations) are

[1]For example, the United Nations rely on only six official languages (United Nations, 2018). The European Commission conducts its internal business in only three procedural languages: English, French, and German (European Commission, 2013)

S. Nothelfer, *Behavior in Foreign Languages*, Innovation und Entrepreneurship,
https://doi.org/10.1007/978-3-658-31853-6_3

particularly globalized. Hence, knowledge of potential foreign language effects on creativity is highly relevant.

We conducted an international experimental study with 430 participants in France, Germany, and the U.S. to observe creative performance in a real-effort creativity task. Participants were randomly assigned to process the task in either their mother tongue or a foreign language. We apply Amabile's (1996) consensual assessment technique to more than 2300 resulting creative products to measure creative performance. Pairwise comparisons across languages allow us to differentiate between foreign language effects and language-specific effects.

Results do not support the existence of a general foreign language effect on creativity. However, we observe a positive language-specific effect on average creativity of processing in German for French native speakers. In addition, we observe performance differences across different countries. Our findings cannot be explained by theories of linguistic relativity, cultural accommodation, or ethnic affirmation.

To our knowledge, this is the first experimental study that examines the impact of foreign language use on creativity in a setting that disentangles a potential foreign language effect from language-specific effects.[2] The study design allows for causal inferences and provides a solid empirical basis for detecting potential foreign language effects on creativity. Our findings contribute to our knowledge of boundaries and relevance of language-induced performance differences. Furthermore, the results demonstrate the importance of investigating several languages and pairings when researching the effects of language use on behavior.

The paper is structured as follows: An initial literature review summarizes and connects theories on the impact of language on behavior and creativity. From this work, we derive two hypotheses on the impact of foreign language use on creativity, which are then tested experimentally. The empirical section first introduces experimental design, subject pool, task, procedures, and creativity assessment. We

---

[2] Haans and van Witteloostuijn (2017) researched language effects on divergent and convergent thinking with Dutch natives who processed in either English or Dutch. They report a positive effect of processing in English for participants with low English language anxiety on convergent thinking, compared to processing in Dutch. The effect turns around for participants with high English language anxiety. However, the experimental design leaves room for alternative explanations. First of all, the researchers cannot differentiate between a possible general foreign language effect, and language-specific effects of processing in English for native speakers of Dutch. Furthermore, the applied unusual uses test for divergent thinking and remote associates test for convergent thinking are text-based. Given that effects only show with language anxiety as a moderator, the results may to some degree only reflect differences in ability. While the study of Haans and van Witteloostuijn (2017) is an interesting contribution to link anxiety to two sub-aspects of creativity, a research gap remains in the question of how processing in foreign languages affects creativity.

then conduct balance checks before proceeding to the main analysis, results, and a concluding discussion.

3.2 Theory

Processing in a foreign language may trigger several effects on behavior simultaneously. By linking theory of potential language effects to creativity theory, we can derive two hypothesis of potential language-induced effects on creativity. The following paragraphs summarize theories on language-specific effects, foreign language effects, and creativity.

3.2.1 Language-Related Effects

It is essential to distinguish between possible language-specific effects and foreign language effects. Both types of effects may be in place simultaneously and overlap.

Language-Specific Effects

Language-specific effects may be caused by characteristics of the used language or by cultural differences between one's own culture and the culture associated with a foreign language. They are generally a function of the specific foreign processing language, and can also depend on an individual's mother tongue (see Chapter 2).

The concept of linguistic relativity assumes that language structure and lexica determine thought through different conceptualizations of time, space, shapes, color, etc. (Boroditsky, 2001; 2003; Everett, 2013; Anthanasopoulos & Aveledo, 2013; Kay & Kempton, 1984). Empirical support for linguistic relativity on intertemporal choice has been reported by Chen (2013) and Sutter, Angerer, Rützler, and Lergetporer (2015).

The conflicting theories of cultural accommodation and ethnic affirmation explain language-specific effects on behavior with cultural differences. Ethnic affirmation, on the one hand, assumes that communicating in a foreign language increases the salience of one's own culture—ultimately resulting in behavior that is more typical for one's own culture (Yang & Bond, 1980; Bond & Yang, 1982). Cultural accommodation, on the other hand, assumes that people accommodate to the culture associated with the foreign language, ultimately adapting their behavior to the foreign culture (Harzing & Maznevski, 2002; Akkermans, Harzing, &

Van Witteloostuijn, 2010; Marian & Kaushanskaya, 2004). In the context of foreign language use, linguistic relativity can be regarded as a particular mechanism that drives cultural accommodation (see Chapter 2).

Foreign Language Effects

Foreign language effects are independent of the specific language used or the culture associated with that language. The use of a foreign language appears to reduce decision biases (Keysar et al. 2012; Costa et al. 2014a). Furthermore, foreign language use has been observed to result in more utilitarian behavior in trolley dilemmas (Costa et al., 2014b; Cipolletti, McFarlane, & Weissglass, 2016; Corey et al., 2017), seems to affect moral judgment (Geipel, Hadjichristidis, & Surian, 2015), and increase freeriding (Urbig et al., 2016). The exact mechanisms leading to such foreign language effects are still subject of debate. In a dual process framework of cognitive processing, foreign language effects are often explained with a shift from intuitive type 1 processing to deliberate type 2 processing. While some assume an actual increase in deliberate type 2 thinking (e.g. Cipolletti et al., 2016; Urbig et al., 2016), more convincing studies suggest a blunted intuition or reduced type 1 processing without increased deliberation as the mechanism (e.g. Hayakawa et al., 2017; Costa et al., 2014a; Geipel, Hadjichristidis, & Surian, 2016). A reduction of intuitive type 1 processing could be related to a decreasing effect of foreign language use on emotional resonance, since it has been shown that foreign language use reduces emotional resonance (Pavlenko, 2005; Dewaele, 2004; 2010; Bond & Lai, 1986; Harris, Aycicegi, & Gleason, 2003; Caldwell-Harris & Aycicegi-Dinn, 2009). Research by Hadjichristidis, Geipel, and Savadori (2015) as well as by Wu and Thierry (2012a) suggests that such a reduced emotional resonance caused by foreign language use may apply to negative emotions only.

Furthermore, foreign language use may influence the retrieval of memory. Episodic memory, which stores events, experiences, and their linguistic environment, is believed to be encoded in a linguistic context. Accordingly, episodic memories are retrieved more easily in a congruent linguistic context, i.e., the language of encoding is identical to the language of retrieval. (Bartolotti & Marian, 2013; Marian & Neisser, 2000; Schrauf & Rubin, 1998; 2000). Semantic memory, which stores general facts, is believed to be language-independent (Bartolotti & Marian, 2013; Szmalec, Brysbaert, & Duyck, 2005; Morford et al., 2011; Shook & Marian, 2012). According to Kroll and Tokowicz (2005), compound bilinguals (who learn two languages simultaneous in the same learning environment) are likely to have one and the same memory system for both languages, while coordinate bilinguals (who learn two languages in strictly separated learning environments or subsequently) have a separate set of concepts/system for each language. Should this be correct, one would expect an improved retrieval of memories when the processing language matches the mother tongue for coordinate bilinguals, and no such effect for compound bilinguals.

3.2.2 Creativity

Creativity is an important aspect of innovation, and individuals often conduct creative work in foreign language settings. A creative outcome is generally seen as something that is both novel and useful (e.g., Plucker & Makel, 2010; Runco, 2007; Amabile, 1996; Sternberg & Lubart, 1996). While this general definition of creativity is widely accepted, a variety of different models aim at explaining the process that leads to creative outcomes.

A large share of creativity research applies simple models of specific thinking patterns. These patterns usually describe one of several possible paths to generate novel ideas. Examples are divergent thinking (Guilford, 1950 as cited in Runco, 2007), overcoming functional fixedness (Duncker & Lees, 1945; Adamson, 1952; Amabile, 1996), analogies (Gick & Holyoak, 1980), or remote associates (Mednick 1962). While such models can be seen as important cognitive building blocks in the creative process, they fail to serve as a comprehensive theory of the creative process (Nothelfer, 2017). Notable models that address the entire creative process are Amabile's (1996) componential framework of creativity, Csikszentmihalyi's (2014) systems perspective, Sternberg's and Lubart's (1996) investment theory, or the geneplore model developed by Finke, Ward, and Smith (1992). The latter models attempt to decompose the creative process and describe it in subsequent steps or iterations. Furthermore, they take into account the environmental context that a creator and her creative product are embedded in.

Linking language-related effects to creativity theory, reduced emotional resonance and reduced access to memory as foreign language effects can be expected to influence creativity. Furthermore, the cultural context may play an important role triggering language-specific effects.

Emotional Resonance

Emotions may influence creative performance. Positive affect can enhance creative performance in Dunker's (1945) candle task and the remote associates test (RAT; Isen, Daubman, & Nowicki, 1987). It appears to increase cognitive flexibility (e.g., Ashby, Valentin, & Turken, 2002; DeDreu, Baas, & Nijstadt, 2008;

Hirt, Devers, & McCrea, 2008), and, when it is activating, creative fluency and originality (DeDreu et al., 2008). Emotional ambivalence has been observed to enhance creativity (Fong, 2006). Negative emotions may also positively affect creative problem solving (Kaufmann & Vosburg, 1997), and, when activating, on creative fluency and originality (DeDreu et al., 2008). However, the latter creativity-increasing effect of negative mood appears to be limited to mood states with a promotion focus and may be reversed in negative mood states with a prevention focus (Baas, DeDreu, & Nijstadt, 2008; George & Zhou, 2002). Overall, most emotions appear to enhance creative performance. A reduced emotional resonance as likely caused by foreign language use is therefore expected to negatively influence creativity.

Memory Access
Memory can be regarded as a common basis for creativity across cognitive building blocks and theories. Our brain relies on memories, and there needs to be some existing experiences, ideas, or concepts to create from. Cognitive building blocks of creativity like remote associates (Mednick, 1962) or analogies are based on connecting previously unconnected concepts, which are stored in memory. It seems likely that existing knowledge, skills, and social norms are at least partly retrieved from episodic memory. Reduced retrieval of memory that may be caused by foreign language use seems therefore likely to negatively influence creativity.

Culture
Creativity could be dependent on culture. Both criteria of novelty and usefulness may be applied differently across cultures (Lubart, 2010; Niu & Sternberg, 2001; Kaufman & Sternberg, 2006), which would influence the perceived creativity of an outcome. Also, some creativity models, such as Csikszentmihalyi's (2014) systems perspective, strongly rely on the cultural context of a creator, which would influence the creative outcome itself. If a creativity-culture relationship existed, language-specific effects related to culture should affect creativity. Thus, cultural accommodation and ethnic affirmation can be adapted to the context of creative performance. Moreover, the culture in which creativity is assessed may influence the assessment.

3.2.3 Hypotheses

Based on the links between language use and creativity, we expect the following relationships:

1. *The use of a foreign language has a negative influence on creativity.*
2. *Language-specific effects can lead to differences in creative performance. Should the culture associated with a foreign language be more (less) creative than the native culture, use of that foreign language can have a positive (negative) influence on creativity.*

The first hypothesis predicts a general foreign language effect on creativity. It is based on a presumed reduced emotional resonance and limited access to memory in foreign language settings as underlying mechanisms. The second hypothesis accounts for possible language-specific effects on creativity, that could be due to cultural accommodation (including linguistic relativity), or ethnic affirmation. The direction of the effect is formulated for cultural accommodation; it should be inverse for ethnic affirmation. While both hypotheses are rooted in theory, our research is to some degree exploratory. The mechanisms behind other observed foreign language effects are not yet fully understood, and creativity theory is too fragmented to derive firm predictions. Looking for empirical evidence, we explore the impact of language on creativity in a series of identical experiments across three countries with varying processing languages.

3.3 Experimental Design

We investigate foreign language effects on creativity with identical experiments in France, Germany, and the United States. Subjects have produced a total of 2307 creative illustrations of objects in an incentivized real-effort task, initially designed by Laske and Schröder (2017). Creative performance is measured subjectively with impartial ratings, applying Amabile's (1996) consensual assessment technique (CAT).

Participants process the experiment in either their mother tongue or a foreign language (random assignment). We make use of an incomplete[3] three-by-three factorial design with the factors mother tongue (French, German, English) and processing language (French, German, English). Data from seven different combinations of mother tongue and processing language allows us to distinguish between language-specific effects and a general foreign language effect (see

[3]While a complete three-by-three experimental design would have been slightly more informative, seven cells are sufficient to disentangle the potential effects (Chapter 2). The chosen incomplete design allows us to use our resources most efficiently, considering the operative effort of experimental data collection at multiple locations.

Chapter 2). Furthermore, the setup supports pair-wise comparisons across processing languages and mother tongues (e.g., German native speakers who process the tasks in German or English compared to English native speakers who process the tasks in English or German).

The assignment between mother tongue and foreign language is fully randomized across the entire sample, while the assignment to a specific processing language is random within cross-pairings of languages[4]. Accordingly, inferences on foreign language effects can be drawn from a larger sample than inferences on language-specific effects.

The between-subjects design has been chosen to rule out learning effects. Moreover, participants in each experimental session were split equally into treatment and control groups to cope with unwanted session-specific effects. A custom-built mobile laboratory was used for the data collection and ensured a comparable laboratory environment across all locations (see Appendix D).

Table 3.1 Number of participants per cell in the incomplete 3 × 3 factorial design

Mother Tongue ▷ *Processing in* ▽	**French**	**German**	**English**	Total
French	44*	54	-	98
German	39	107*	64	210
English	-	58	64*	122
Total	83	219	128	**430**

* Control, mother tongue

_ Treatment, foreign language

3.3.1 Subject Pool

In order to ensure a sufficient language proficiency and for comparability across countries, all participants were recruited from university language programs. Participant had to be bilingual at the CEFR proficiency level of B2[5] or above to ensure a full understanding of the tasks.

A total of 469 students from seven universities in Germany, the United States, and France participated in the study (see Appendix B.1 for details). 39 participants, whose mother tongue structure prevented a random assignment into the

[4]In cross-pairings, two languages serve as both mother tongue and foreign language. For example, French native speakers process in French or in German, and German native speakers process in French or in German.

[5]In the common European framework of reference for languages, B2 refers to an upper intermediate level.

treatment or control group, were excluded from analysis. Excluded participants either had a mother tongue that was neither the treatment nor the control language (which would always assign them to the treatment group), or multiple mother tongues that included both treatment and control language (which would always assign them to the control group). The remaining subject pool consists of 430 participants.

Table 3.1 provides an overview of the subject structure. As all sessions were equally split between treatment and control, and German was compared to both English and French, the number of participants with German mother tongue processing in German is considerably higher than the other groups.

3.3.2 Procedure

Potential subjects were informed that participation in the study was voluntary and did not affect their grades in any way.

Our specifically built mobile laboratory was set up in suitable seminar rooms or classrooms at each location. The lab consists of adapted tablet devices, a specifically designed closed-network infrastructure with Daphne and Apache servers, experiment-specific materials, and testing dividers. Experiments were programmed as apps relying on the open-source platform oTree (Chen, Schonger, & Wickens, 2014) and web-development tools (Django, Bootstrap, Ajax). More detailed information on the laboratory is provided in Appendix D.

Half the seats in the laboratory room were prepared for treatment and half for control. Using a seat number lottery, participants were randomly assigned to process the study either in their mother tongue (control) or the foreign language (treatment). The seat assignment took place before participants entered the room. Subjects were not made aware of the nature of the treatment.

All materials and all instructions were provided in the assigned language. In order to ensure consistency, they were translated and back-translated from German (Brislin 1970). Testing dividers and the seat arrangement ensured that participants could not spot any material in a language different from their own material. A bilingual experimenter answered questions individually and quietly in the assigned language.

After completing the experiments, all participants received a show-up fee of 6 €/$ plus additional variable payments from the incentivized tasks. The show-up fee was paid in cash immediately after the session. Payments for the incentivized tasks were made about four weeks later, in order to run subsequent rating sessions to determine payoffs.

3.3.3 Task

Participants received a series of three experimental tasks with coupled priming tasks in the assigned language, followed by a questionnaire in their mother tongue. This study is based exclusively on data from the one of these three experiments that addresses creativity. In order to account for potential order effects between the three tasks, task order was varied across sessions in a 3×3 latin-square permutation.

The initial priming task was intended to strengthen the cognitive presence of the assigned language. Participants wrote out a given short text on a sheet of paper. The text was chosen to be fully comprehensible for B2 proficiency levels and emotion-neutral. Following this text reproduction, participants received a reflection question on the content of the text.

Subsequent to the priming came a real-effort task to create several individual creative products. Subjects were instructed to illustrate objects of their choice with a given set of material, then photograph and submit each illustration with the tablet device. Subjects were informed that all submitted illustrations would be rated on creativity, technical goodness, and aesthetics by an international jury after the experiment. Creativity was incentivized. Each participant's three highest rated illustrations determined their payoff for this task, theoretically ranging from 0.60 €/$ to 5.40 €/$. Appendix B.4 contains the instructions in English.

Several control questions with immediate feedback were asked to ensure that the participants understood the task. Participants then had three minutes to practice taking pictures and submitting them with the tablet device before proceeding to the illustration task.

Within ten minutes, participants were asked to create, photograph and submit as many illustrations of objects as they liked. Subjects learned the exact content of the set of material only immediately before the start of the ten minutes. The remaining time was visualized with a counter. The illustration task including the choice of provided material was originally designed by Laske & Schröder (2017). While all instructions were provided in either treatment or control language, the task itself was purposely chosen to be purely graphical and thus independent of language. Figure 3.1 contains an exemplary illustration and shows the given set of material.

Figure 3.1 Example illustration and the given set of material

3.3.4 Creativity Assessment

Based on the illustrations as creative products, creativity is measured subjectively with Amabile's (1996) consensual assessment technique (CAT). Each illustrated object was rated by six raters on 9-point discrete visual analog scales on creativity, quality of the technical execution, and aesthetic appeal. The latter two factors have previously been found to be orthogonal to creativity (Amabile 1996) and were included to isolate creativity. In our sample, we find strong correlations between ratings on creativity and technical goodness (coefficient 0.62), as well as between ratings on creativity and aesthetic appeal (coefficient 0.61). These correlations indicate that the raters may not have fully distinguished between the three factors.

The CAT generally relies on the rating of expert judges. Since the chosen task cannot be associated with one clear domain of expertise, our measures rely on novice raters that were trained before the rating, as discussed by Kaufman, Baer, and Cole (2006).

In order to account for potential cultural differences across raters, and cultural interactions between rater and illustration, each illustration was rated by two raters from each Germany, the U.S., and France. Illustrations were rated in six bulks for operational reasons and randomly assigned to raters within each bulk. An algorithm ensured that no illustration was assigned to the same rater twice. Despite the clustering in bulks, all raters were randomly drawn from the same subject pools in France, Germany, and the United States. Raters were registered to ensure that no rater could participate in the online rating more than once. More details on rater structure, rating procedures, and an analysis of rating behavior across rating groups can be found in Appendix B.2.

Ratings were conducted with a total of 312 raters in online sessions in the prevalent language of the rater pool's country. All instructions were translated and back-translated from German in order to ensure equivalence (Brislin 1970). Raters received an explanation of the illustrator's task, followed by 20 randomly selected example illustrations to familiarize them with the task and provide them with references (training). Subsequently, each rater rated between 47 and 50 randomly assigned illustrations on 9-point scales on creativity, quality of the technical execution, and aesthetic appeal. Our algorithm ensured that the illustrations to be rated were different from the previously shown examples. Inter-rater reliability was measured conservatively with a (1,6) intra-class correlation in accordance with Shrout and Fleiss (1979). A resulting average coefficient of 0.70 (95% confidence interval from 0.69 to 0.72) indicates a fair degree of rater agreement.

While we furthermore analyze the number of illustrations that were produced in the given time (fluency), it should be noted that fluency is not a suitable measure for creative performance in our setting, as fluency was not incentivized (see "Task").

3.4 Dataset and Balance Checks

The 430 participants in our sample created a total of 2307 illustrations[6]. Each illustration was rated by six raters, leaving us with a total of 13842 observations. Table 3.2 provides an overview of the dataset.

Table 3.2 Descriptive statistics of the dataset

	Total		Foreign language		Mother tongue		German MT		French MT		English MT	
Participants	430		215		215		219		84†		128†	
Illustrations	2307		1149		1158		1252		395†		663†	
	mean	*sd*	*mean*	*sd*	*mean*	*sd*	*mean*	*sd*	*mean*	*sd*	*mean*	*sd*
Age	22,80	5,97	22,49	5,33	23,1	6,54	22,86	5,15	23,54	8,15	22,16	5,54
Female	0,65	0,48	0,66	0,48	0,64	0,48	0,73	0,45	0,65	0,48	0,52***	0,50
Proficiency in fl	4,13	0.92	4,13	0,86	4,13	0,98	4,32	0,92	4,12*	0,84	3,81***	0,88
Abroad experience in fl	0,63	0,48	0,63	0,48	0,64	0,48	0,62	0,49	0,75**	0,44	0,59	0,49
Illustrations per participant	5,37	2,27	5,34	2,43	5,39	2,09	5,72	2,38	4,70***	1,80	5,18**	2,25
Creativity of illustrations, all	5,03	1,48	5,28	1,47	5,04	1,57	5,07	1,54	5,16	1,51	5,31*	1,88
Creativity of illustrations, top 3	5,87	1,17	5,89	1,16	5,84	1,18	5,93	1,16	5,66***	1,17	5,88	1,16
Creativity of illustrations, top 1	6,64	0,98	6,67	0,97	6,60	0,99	6,72	0,93	6,40***	0,96	6,65	1,04

All differences between Foreign language / Mother tongue are statistically insignificant. Stars indicate differences between groups of French and English mother tongues compared to German mother tongue (t-test). *** $p<0.01$, ** $p<0.05$, * $p<0.1$

† including one participant with both French and English mother tongue

[6]Three photos of illustrations were plainly black and therefore removed from the dataset.

Comparisons between subjects in the foreign language (treatment) and the mother tongue (control) groups show similar means and no significant differences (t-tests) in age, gender, self-reported foreign language proficiency, or abroad experience (i.e., having lived in a country of the foreign treatment language). This indicates that the random assignment to either treatment or control was successful.

Comparisons of groups of mother tongues show significant differences in gender and foreign language proficiency between participants of English and German mother tongues, and significant differences in foreign language proficiency and abroad experience between participants of French and German mother tongues. Due to the randomization within each session, these differences are irrelevant for the analysis of a foreign language effect. Nevertheless, they may affect the identification of potential language-specific effects. Therefore, gender, proficiency and abroad experience are controlled for in Appendix B.3.

Participants submitted an average of 5.37 illustrations (SD 2.27). Participants of German mother tongue on average submitted significantly more images that participants of English or French mother tongues. On this aggregate level, comparisons between the foreign language treatment and the control group indicate no statistically significant differences with regards to creativity scores or amounts of images per participant.

The mean creativity score for all images is lowest for participants of German mother tongue and highest for participants of English mother tongue. Taking into account each participant's, top 3 and top 1 highest rated illustrations, participants of German mother tongue on average show the highest scores, and participants of French mother tongue show the lowest. This pattern has led us to further investigate the relationship between the number of illustrations per participant and creativity ratings.

3.5 Analysis and Results

In the following paragraphs, we analyze creativity scores of all illustrations, of each participant's top 3 highest ranked illustrations, and of each participant's top 1 highest ranked illustration. While the top 3 illustrations were incentivized, most participants submitted more illustrations, not knowing which of their submissions would end up among the top 3. The top 1 illustrations are particularly interesting in the context of innovation, which often relies on the best ideas only (Girotra, Terwiesch & Ulrich, 2018, Dahan & Mendelson 2001). In addition, the relationship between the number of illustrations and creativity scores is discussed and analyzed.

For our analysis, we conduct regressions on several models to identify potential effects. We start with a simple model type "a" to detect overall foreign language effects. By adding dummy variables for mother tongues in models "b" and interactions between mother tongues and foreign language treatment in models "c", we achieve a more detailed picture. Comparisons across the models help us to differentiate between language-specific effects and general foreign language effects.

Our primary dependent variables are individual creativity scores made on a scale from 1 (low) to 9 (high). In the following models, Y_{ijk} denotes the creativity score for illustration j of participant i and rater k.

Model type "a"

$$Y_{ijk} = \beta_0 + \beta_1 * fl_i + e_{ijk}$$

Baseline in models named with the letter "a" are participants that process in their mother tongue. The independent variable *fl* is a dummy for processing in a foreign language.

Model type "b"

$$Y_{ijk} = \beta_0 + \beta_1 * fl_i + \beta_2 * mten_i + \beta_3 * mtfr_i + e_{ijk}$$

Model type "b" adds dummy variables for English mother tongue (*mten*) and French mother tongue (*mtfr*) to model "a". Accordingly, the baseline are participants of German mother tongue who process in German.

Model type "c"

$$Y_{ijk} = \beta_0 + \beta_1 * fl_i + \beta_2 * mten_i + \beta_3 * mtfr_i + \beta_4 * fl_i * mten_i + \beta_5 * fl_i * mtfr_i + e_{ijk}$$

Model type "c" adds interactions between foreign language processing and mother tongues to model "b" (*fl*mten*, *fl*mtfr*). The baseline are German native speakers who process in German. Due to these interactions, β_1 estimates the effect of processing in French or English for participants of German mother tongue only. β_2 estimates the effect of having an English mother tongue and processing in English, compared to the baseline (β_3 is analogous for French). The sums ($\beta_1 + \beta_4$) and ($\beta_1 + \beta_5$) estimate the effect for processing in German for participants of English and French mother tongues, compared to the baseline.

In our regressions on creativity scores, we cluster standard errors on participants and raters. Individual raters may be subject to different anchor points and usage of the rating scale. However, we cannot include rater fixed effects in the main regression due to the assignment of raters in bulks. Individual raters are uncorrelated with the foreign language treatment, but correlations exist between individual raters and subject pools. Nevertheless, our estimates should be unbiased, since raters were randomly drawn from identical pools in a short timespan, no rater could rate in more than one session, and illustrations were randomly assigned to raters within each bulk. Further analysis of ratings in Appendix B.2.3 and regressions within groups separated by mother tongues that allow us to include rater fixed effects (Appendix B.3.1) lead to consistent results and support the absence of systematic differences of rater pools across bulks.

In the following paragraphs, we first present some general results of regression analysis, before proceeding to robustness checks and an analysis of the relationship between fluency and creativity. Table 3.3, Table 3.4, and Table 3.5 show OLS regressions with two-way clustering on participants and raters. Due to potential influences by different task orders within the series of experiments, our robustness check includes additional regressions on a sub-pool of participants that received the creativity task first.

3.5.1 Regression Analysis

When analyzing the creativity scores of all 430 participants with OLS regressions, results do not support a general foreign language effect on creativity (Table 3.3). However, a positive effect of processing in German appears to be in place for participants of French mother tongue.

3.5.1.1 All Illustrations

When taking into account all illustrations that were submitted (models 1a-c), we observe a significantly different foreign language effect for participants with French as their mother tongue who process in German as a foreign language (*fl*mtfr* in model 1c) compared to Germans who process in a foreign language. A Wald test for joint significance of *fl*mtfr* and *fl* in model 1c shows, that processing in German appears to have a significantly positive overall impact on creative performance for participants of French mother tongue ($p = 0.031$).

The coefficient for participants of German mother tongue who process in either French or English as a foreign language is negative, but not significant (*fl* in model 1c). Coefficients of almost 0 for *fl* in models 1a-b and differences in the sign of foreign language coefficients (*fl* vs. *fl* + *fl**mten* vs. *fl* + *fl**mtfr*) in model 1c speak against a general foreign language effect on creativity.

Furthermore, processing in German does not seem to affect participants of English mother tongue (*fl* + *fl**mten* in model 1c, Wald test $p = 0.689$).

Coefficients for groups that process in their mother tongues (*mten, mtfr* in model 1c) indicate potential cultural differences between French and German participants (*mtfr* is negative in 1c, but not significant). No cultural differences seem to be in place between participants of German and English mother tongues. The observed pattern is therefore in line with the theory of cultural accommodation and contradicts ethnic affirmation.

Table 3.3 OLS regressions on the creative performance of all participants

VARIABLES	(1a) crea_all	(1b) crea_all	(1c) crea_all	(2a) crea_top3	(2b) crea_top3	(2c) crea_top3	(3a) crea_top1	(3b) crea_top1	(3c) crea_top1
fl	-0.037	-0.034	-0.212	0.047	0.040	-0.027	0.070	0.061	-0.013
	(0.096)	(0.094)	(0.143)	(0.085)	(0.085)	(0.119)	(0.090)	(0.089)	(0.120)
mten		0.139	0.007		-0.049	-0.086		-0.070	-0.149
		(0.152)	(0.174)		(0.149)	(0.180)		(0.152)	(0.190)
mtfr		0.042	-0.242		-0.277*	-0.386**		-0.317*	-0.384**
		(0.168)	(0.200)		(0.158)	(0.190)		(0.167)	(0.187)
fl*mten			0.265			0.075			0.158
			(0.194)			(0.189)			(0.204)
fl*mtfr			0.598***			0.231			0.139
			(0.228)			(0.223)			(0.236)
Constant	5.047***	4.998***	5.090***	5.843***	5.914***	5.948***	6.603***	6.690***	6.728***
	(0.080)	(0.101)	(0.111)	(0.081)	(0.099)	(0.108)	(0.082)	(0.098)	(0.104)
Observations	13,842	13,842	13,842	7,548	7,548	7,548	2,580	2,580	2,580
R-squared	0.000	0.001	0.003	0.000	0.003	0.003	0.000	0.004	0.005

OLS regression.Robust standard errors clustered on raters and creators in parentheses.
*** p<0.01, ** p<0.05, * p<0.1

3.5.1.2 Highest-Ranked Illustrations

Analyzing the creativity ratings of the highest ranked illustrations (top 1 and top 3; models 2a-3c) does not support a general foreign language effect on creativity (coefficients for *fl* are almost 0 in models 2a-b and 3a-b).

Coefficients for *fl**mtfr* in models 2c and 3c are of considerable size and positive, but not statistically significant, as opposed to the analysis of all illustrations. Wald tests for joint significance of *fl* + *fl**mtfr* in models 2c ($p = 0.288$) and 3c ($p = 0.538$) reveal no significant language-specific effect of processing in German for participants of French mother tongue. Analogously, no effect of processing in German for participants of English mother tongue can be observed (Wald test *fl* + *fl**mten*, $p = 0.745$ in model 2c, $p = 0.383$ in model 3c). Likewise, for participants of German mother tongue, foreign language processing does not seem to affect creativity ratings of top 3 (*fl* in model 2c) and top 1 (*fl* in model 3c) highest rated illustrations.

Participants of French mother tongue performed significantly worse than participants of German mother tongue (*mtfr* in models 2c and 3c). In this setting, cultural accommodation would predict a positive effect of German processing for participants of French mother tongue, and a negative effect of French processing for participants of German mother tongue. The absence of significant effects for participants of German mother tongue speaks against cultural accommodation. Furthermore, the patterns are not in line with ethnic affirmation.

3.5.2 Robustness

Controlling for rater fixed effects (Appendix B.3.1) supports the absence of a foreign language effect in our data. Separate analyses of sub-groups by combinations of mother tongue/treatment language confirms the positive effect of processing in German for participants of French mother tongue on the average creativity of all illustrations (Appendix B.3, model 9). In addition, there appears to be a marginally significant negative effect of processing in French for participants of German mother tongue on the creativity of the top 1 highest ranked illustration when including rater fixed effects (Appendix B.3, model 14b).

When controlling for gender, proficiency, abroad experience, and task order within the experimental series, the observed pattern from Table 3.3 persists (Appendix B.3, models 1a_ctr–6c_ctr). Gender appears to influence creative performance, as female participants scored significantly higher than males on the top 3 and top 1 highest ranked illustrations. In addition, the task order of the creativity task within the series of three different tasks appears to matter. Processing the creativity task in second or third position after other tasks positively affects creativity scores.

In order to account for possible confounding effects from having previously processed another experimental task, we analyze a subset of data from participants that received the creativity task first. In our latin-square permutation of task orders, this accounts for roughly a third of the total data ($n = 155$). The subset shares the characteristics of the full dataset regarding subject pools and randomization.

Table 3.4 shows the same OLS regressions as in Table 3.3, conducted in the reduced dataset from participants who received the creativity task first.

Compared to the full dataset, coefficients for foreign language processing appear to be more positive overall. Significantly positive coefficients for *fl* in models 6a-b indicate a potential positive foreign language effect on creativity. However, this effect seems to be primarily driven by participants of French mother tongue who process in German.

Table 3.4 OLS regressions on the creative performance of 155 participants that received the creativity task first

VARIABLES	(4a) crea_all	(4b) crea_all	(4c) crea_all	(5a) crea_top3	(5b) crea_top3	(5c) crea_top3	(6a) crea_top1	(6b) crea_top1	(6c) crea_top1
fl	0.254	0.236	0.178	0.235	0.206	0.141	0.320**	0.290*	0.138
	(0.172)	(0.173)	(0.262)	(0.148)	(0.147)	(0.208)	(0.163)	(0.163)	(0.225)
mten		0.142	0.277		-0.013	0.033		0.002	-0.108
		(0.222)	(0.298)		(0.205)	(0.276)		(0.228)	(0.315)
mtfr		-0.124	-0.378		-0.373*	-0.547**		-0.345	-0.543**
		(0.220)	(0.259)		(0.202)	(0.245)		(0.215)	(0.268)
fl*mten			-0.249			-0.070			0.221
			(0.376)			(0.344)			(0.370)
fl*mtfr			0.675*			0.415			0.458
			(0.365)			(0.338)			(0.408)
Constant	4.834***	4.830***	4.857***	5.698***	5.793***	5.824***	6.412***	6.498***	6.575***
	(0.130)	(0.170)	(0.194)	(0.123)	(0.152)	(0.170)	(0.132)	(0.157)	(0.171)
Observations	4,794	4,794	4,794	2,682	2,682	2,682	930	930	930
R-squared	0.003	0.004	0.008	0.003	0.008	0.009	0.006	0.011	0.013

OLS regression.Robust standard errors clustered on raters and creators in parentheses.
*** p<0.01, ** p<0.05, * p<0.1

The previously observed pattern regarding positive effects of German processing for participants of French mother tongue persists and is even stronger (Wald tests *fl* + *fl*mtfr*; p = 0.001 in model 4c; p = 0.040 in model 5c; p = 0.085 in model 6c). Coefficients for foreign language processing for participants of German mother tongue are positive, but insignificant (*fl*, p = 0.496 in model 4c; p = 0.497 in model 5c; p = 0.540). Coefficients for participants of English mother tongue who process in German are insignificant, and even negative when taking into account all illustrations (Wald tests *fl* + *fl*mten*; p = 0.798 in model 4c; p = 0.800 in model 5c; p = 0.235 in model 6c).

Accordingly, the pattern appears to support a positive language-specific effect of German processing for participants of French mother tongue more than a general foreign language effect.

Consistent with the full dataset, the subset reveals cultural differences between participants of German and French mother tongues (*mtfr* in models 4c, 5c, 6c). While the significantly positive effect of German processing for participants of French mother tongue is in line with cultural accommodation, a positive direction of the *fl* coefficient in models 5c, and 6c speaks against the theory of cultural accommodation. Instead, it seems more likely that the observed language-specific effect has other causes. Its direction in line with cultural accommodation could be pure coincidence.

When controlling for gender, proficiency, and abroad experience in the reduced subject pool the overall pattern persists (Appendix B.3.4).

3.5.3 Relationship between Fluency and Creativity Scores

The number of illustrations submitted by each participant may be referred to as creative fluency. While fluency is often used as a measure of creative performance, it was not an incentivized goal in our setting. Hence, we cannot determine whether potential differences in fluency reflect lower creative ability, or conscious decisions by participants. However, due to significant differences in fluency between the subject pools of different countries, we investigate the relationship between fluency and creativity in the following paragraphs.

In our study, fluency and creativity scores could be interrelated in two opposing ways:

Firstly, assuming that spending more time illustrating a single object leads to a more creative illustration, we would expect a tradeoff between fluency and creativity scores in settings with limited time.

Secondly, assuming that creativity scores across each individual's illustrations are subject to unexplained variance including rater error, a higher amount of images should on average lead to higher top 3 and top 1 creativity scores.

Our data support a possible tradeoff between fluency and creativity scores. We observe a negative correlation of -0.38 ($p<0.001$) between the mean creativity score across all images per participant and the number of images per participant. When correlating the number of images with the average creativity rating of the top 3 and top 1 illustrations, we observe slightly positive coefficient of 0.087 ($p = 0.072$) for top 3 illustrations, and almost no correlation for top 1 illustrations (coefficient 0.017, $p = 0.727$) (Figure 3.2). The absence of a correlation between fluency and creativity for the highest ranked illustration, in combination with the generally negative correlation for all illustration, suggests that both interrelationships between fluency and creativity scores are in place simultaneously. The possible positive effect of fluency on creativity scores due to variance in ratings appears to counterbalance the adverse effect of investing less time per illustration.

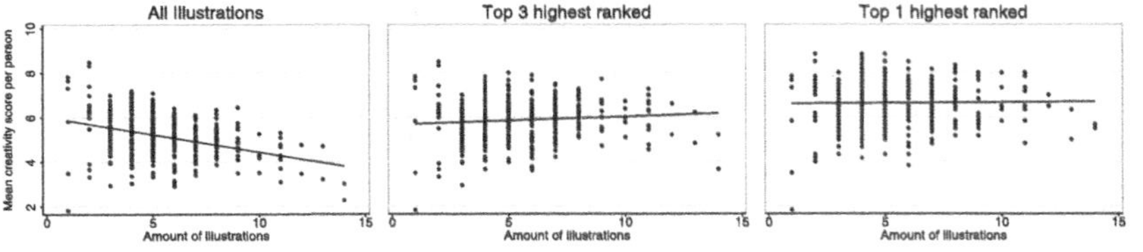

Figure 3.2 Relationship between fluency and creativity

3.5.3.1 Strategies

In the experimental task, participants were given ten minutes to illustrate as many objects as they liked. Only the creativity scores of the top 3 determined the payoff. The relationship between fluency and creativity scores gives room for different strategies.

On one extreme side, one could merely illustrate as many objects as possible. This strategy seems favorable if the creativity ratings are subject to high uncertainty. Some possible sources of uncertainty are rating error, different conceptualizations of creativity between individual raters, or even a lack of confidence of the creator about judging the creativity of their own illustrations.

On the other extreme, one could spend the entire time on only three illustrations, attempting to maximize their creativity. Maximizing the creative quality of only three illustrations seems a favorable strategy if the uncertainty of creativity ratings is low. This implies a confident assumption of what the raters will see as creative.

Figure 3.3 shows the frequencies of the amount of illustrations participants have submitted in foreign language and mother tongue settings. Comparing the total images per person by treatment groups does not reveal a significant difference (t-test $p = 0.848$, Kolmogorov-Smirnov test $p = 0.827$). Furthermore, the distributions do not support the two extreme strategies of either maximizing the quantity or the quality of few illustrations. Instead, most participants have submitted between four and seven illustrations.

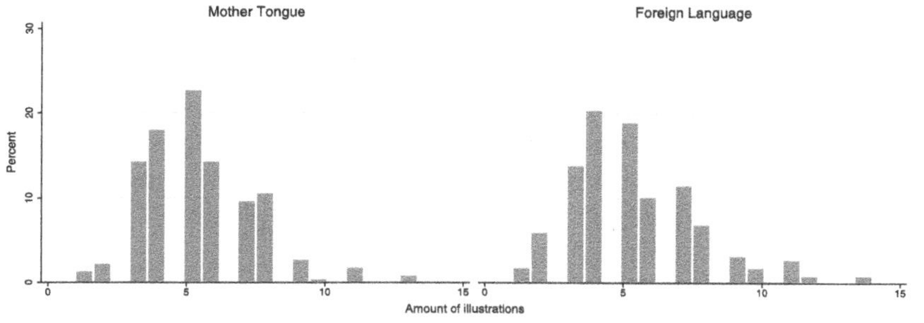

Figure 3.3 Amounts of illustrations per participant by treatment

3.5.3.2 Regressions on Fluency

In the following, we discuss OLS regressions with the amount of illustrations per participant as the dependent variable (Table 3.5). Independent variables including controls are analogous to previous models (see, e.g. Table 3.3).

Table 3.5 OLS regressions on fluency

VARIABLES	(7a) Total Images	(7b) Total Images	(7c) Total Images	(7a_ctr) Total Images	(7b_ctr) Total Images	(7c_ctr) Total Images
fl	-0.042	-0.070	0.127	-0.040	-0.066	0.139
	(0.219)	(0.216)	(0.320)	(0.220)	(0.217)	(0.320)
mten		-0.536**	-0.269		-0.476*	-0.199
		(0.253)	(0.345)		(0.281)	(0.375)
mtfr		-1.017***	-0.919***		-1.008***	-0.904***
		(0.251)	(0.311)		(0.261)	(0.328)
fl*mten			-0.532			-0.547
			(0.507)			(0.507)
fl*mtfr			-0.200			-0.214
			(0.511)			(0.511)
female				0.349	0.271	0.275
				(0.235)	(0.240)	(0.241)
proficiency				0.087	0.022	0.024
				(0.139)	(0.142)	(0.144)
abroad experience				0.049	0.139	0.149
				(0.245)	(0.245)	(0.243)
order crea first				-0.270	-0.272	-0.266
				(0.263)	(0.262)	(0.264)
order crea second				0.149	0.141	0.148
				(0.278)	(0.274)	(0.273)
Constant	5.386***	5.758***	5.659***	4.816***	5.436***	5.307***
	(0.143)	(0.182)	(0.206)	(0.632)	(0.703)	(0.733)
Observations	430	430	430	430	430	430
R-squared	0.000	0.032	0.034	0.012	0.041	0.043

OLS regressions. Robust standard errors clustering for participants in parentheses
*** p<0.01, ** p<0.05, * p<0.1

Results do not support a foreign language effect on fluency. Furthermore, coefficients for foreign language processing in model 7c do not reveal significant effects for any mother tongue (model 7c; *fl*, p = 0.691; Wald test *fl*mten* + *fl*, p = 0.308; Wald test *fl*mtfr* + *fl*, p = 0.856). However, there appears to be some strong cultural differences. Participants of French and English mother tongues have submitted significantly fewer illustrations than participants of German mother tongue (*mtfr, mten* in model 7b). These patterns are robust for controls (models 7a_ctr–7c_ctr).

On average, participants of French mother tongue have submitted one illustration less than participants of German mother tongue. When we take into account the slightly positive correlation between fluency and top 3 creativity scores, the question arises whether this significant difference in fluency might drive the significantly worse creativity scores of French mother tongue participants for their top 3 illustrations (models 2a–2c and 5a–5c).

This does not seem to be the case. Firstly, the correlation between fluency and top 1 creativity scores is almost zero, and participants of French mother tongue also performed significantly worse than the baseline for top 1 illustrations (model 3a–3c and 6a–6c). Secondly, controlling for the number of images in the regression analysis for top 3 and top 1 illustrations leads to similar results as those found in Table 3.3 (see Appendix B.3.2, models 21–23). The effect of worse creative performance for top 3 and top 1 illustrations among participants of French mother tongue cannot be attributed to differences in fluency.

Following the same logic, the positive effect of processing in German for participants of French mother tongue on the average creativity of all illustrations cannot be explained by differences in fluency. The joint coefficient for processing in German for participants of French mother tongue is almost negligible (*fl* + *fl*mtfr* in model 7c). The positive effects on average creativity for participants of French mother tongue who process in German (see models 1a–1c and 4a–4c), in combination with the negative correlation between average creativity and fluency may raise overall robustness questions. Controlling for fluency in the regression on average creativity shows that the positive effect of German processing observed in Table 3.3 persists (see Appendix, B.3.2 model 21), and the previously insignificant negative coefficient for French mother tongue *mtfr* becomes more negative and significant.

3.6 Discussion

What is the impact of foreign language use on creative performance? This paper derives a possible foreign language effect from theory and empirically investigates this question with an international experiment in France, Germany, and the United States.

In an incomplete three-by-three factorial design with the factors mother tongue and processing language, we compared seven different combinations of the languages English, French, and German. Subjects were randomly assigned to process the tasks in either a foreign language (treatment), or their mother tongue (control). Data were collected with incentivized real-effort creativity tasks at seven universities in six cities, and subsequent web-based rating sessions in France, Germany, and the United States. We gathered a statistically meaningful sample of 430 participants, 2307 creative products, and 13842 creativity ratings. Pairwise comparisons of participants with inverted combinations of mother tongue and treatment language allow us to distinguish a possible foreign language effect from language-specific, cultural effects.

First and perhaps most importantly, our empirical results do not support the existence of a general foreign language effect on creativity (hypothesis 1). When taking into account all data and sub-group analyses, coefficients for foreign language processing are often of negligible size, point in different directions, and are without statistical significance.

Secondly, we find evidence for a language-specific effect. For participants of French mother tongue who process in German, we observe a significant positive effect on creativity when looking at all illustrations, and at the top 1 highest-ranked illustrations. The effect is rather robust and appears to be limited to participants of French mother tongue. In the English/German pairing, we do not observe a statistically significant effect of processing in German for participants of English mother tongue. Moreover, processing in either French or English does not seem to have an apparent effect on participants of German mother tongue.

With regards to the theories of cultural accommodation and ethnic affirmation (hypothesis 2), our data strongly contradicts predictions of ethnic affirmation. Evidence for cultural accommodation is mixed. While parts of our data are in line with cultural accommodation, others are not. Language-specific effects for German processing for participants of French mother tongue and corresponding cultural differences are in line with predictions of cultural accommodation. However, as the theoretical predictions by cultural accommodation do not apply to participants of all mother tongues, our data is far from providing solid support for the theory. Pure coincidence is an alternative explanation for the observed consistency. Further empirical research on cultural accommodation that affects only some language combinations would be interesting[7].

Thirdly, we find some evidence for subject pool differences across country borders, that may indicate cross-cultural differences in creativity. The most creative illustrations of participants with French mother tongue appear less creative than those of participants with German mother tongue, regardless of the treatment language. Comparing the observed pattern to the pairing of English and German, we do not observe a statistically significant positive effect of processing in German for participants of English mother tongue. Furthermore, we observe differences in fluency across subject pools. Participants of French or English mother tongue have submitted significantly fewer illustrations than participants of German mother tongue.

Findings are robust when controlling for gender, proficiency, fluency, abroad experience[8], and rater fixed effects in subgroups. By exploring the relationship between fluency and creativity scores, we can conclude that neither the positive effect of processing in German for the average of all illustrations nor the lower scores for the highest ranked illustrations are caused by differences in creative fluency. In our particular task, fluency was not incentivized and should not be interpreted as a measure of creative performance. Yet, we observe two opposite relationships between fluency and creativity scores. On the one hand, there appears to be a tradeoff between fluency and average creativity scores of all illustrations, possibly due to the imposed time restriction. On the other hand, high fluency appears to be of advantage for the creativity scores for highest ranked illustrations, quite possibly due to errors and random variance in ratings.

This paper contributes to literature in several ways. First and foremost, it explores the scope and boundaries of foreign language effects, extending our knowledge on their relevance to the field of creativity. Second, it demonstrates the importance of observing pairings of languages and multiple languages in empirical studies about effects of language use. If we had only tested participants of French mother tongue who process in either French or German, it would have been impossible to tell whether our findings indicate a foreign language effect or a language-specific effect that should not be generalized. Keeping this in mind, empirical studies on

[7]See also Chapter 2

[8]Living abroad has previously found to have a positive effect on creativity (Leung et al., 2008; Maddux & Galinsky, 2009). While we find some support for a positive effect of abroad experiences on the average creativity across all illustrations of a participant, this effect appears to vanish for the top 1 highest ranked illustrations.

language-induced effects, which are based on only one foreign processing language, should be interpreted with extreme caution. Third, to our knowledge, this is the first empirical study that compares creative performance across countries in France, Germany, and the United States. When interpreted with the necessary caution that is due to non-representative subject pools, this paper contributes to the literature of cross-cultural studies.

3.7 Limitations and Outlook

As any empirical study, our experiment comes with limitations.

While comparisons of language pairings are methodologically rigorous, our study is based on combinations of only three commonly used languages. We must keep in mind that we observe only a tiny excerpt from a multitude of possible language combinations. While our sample should be affected by potential general foreign language effects, it is far from comprehensive. The three chosen languages are part of the same Indo-Germanic family, and all subjects belong to the "Western" part of the world. Extending the study to pairings of languages with greater differences, such as Mandarin-French, would be very interesting, although challenging from an operational point of view.

The subject pools were chosen to be similar across countries. Subjects were recruited from language programs at universities in order to ensure a minimum proficiency in the target language. As a consequence, our subjects are likely above average regarding education and intelligence and belong to a relatively narrow age group. Generalizability of our findings to subjects of different demographics cannot be guaranteed. We would argue, though, that many people that frequently interact or work in foreign languages seem likely to share some common ground with our subject pools.

When interpreting this study in a context of cross-cultural research, comparisons across subject pools must be made with the necessary caution. Apart from observing a particular subgroup of each country's population, regional cultural differences within countries are likely not balanced. Clearly, the subject pools are not representative samples of their respective country's societies. However, investigating comparable subject pools from different societies is a common practice in cross-cultural research (Gächter, Herrmann, & Thöni, 2010).

The creativity task in this study is mainly visual and does not include text production. Illustrations have the advantage of being language-independent, eliminating direct and trivial influences of proficiency. On the downside, not all creative work is visual, which may arise potential questions for generalizability. Other creative work, such as creative writing, may interact with specific languages, particularly when considering the concept of linguistic relativity.

Last but not least, creative performance is observed only as a subjectively measurable outcome of behavior. Our experimental design hardly permits to draw any conclusions on underlying cognitive mechanisms related to foreign language use or to the creative process that may be in place.

Looking forward, research in three areas could further advance our understanding of impact of language on behavior.

First, reported foreign language effects of studies relying on data with only one foreign language should be tested with additional foreign languages and mother tongues, ideally producing data that contains language pairings[9]. Without such pairings and multiple languages, it remains speculative whether some of the reported findings of foreign language effects are indeed due to foreign language use, or due to language-specific effects.

Second, extending our study to languages and countries which are more distant from each other would improve the generalizability of our findings and may lead to new insights. Given that our creativity task is visual, research on Mandarin as a logographic language would be particularly interesting.

Third, the observed language-specific effect of processing in German for participants of French mother tongue is a phenomenon that requires further research. An attempt to replicate the findings with different subject pools would be valuable. Moreover, further investigating the role of cultural differences and stereotypes could lead to valuable insights.

[9]A noteworthy study in that direction was conducted by Hayakawa (2017), who successfully replicated findings of a previously reported foreign language effect on moral judgment.

Cooperation in Foreign Languages 4

4.1 Introduction

Human cooperation across different languages and cultures is a cornerstone of our globalized world. It is of vital importance for international politics, international business, science, or any organization with cross-national teams. The question arises as to whether cross-cultural and cross-linguistic cooperative behavior differ systematically from cooperative behavior within the same language and culture. While individual cooperation across cultures has been researched extensively (see, e.g., Gächter, Herrmann, & Thöni, 2010; Dorrough & Glöckner, 2016; Wong & Hong, 2005), our knowledge of the role of different languages is sparse. Processing in a foreign language has been shown to shape individuals' decisions in other domains. For example, it affects risky decision making (Keysar, Hayakawa, & An, 2012, Costa et al. 2014a), and utilitarian vs. deontological decision making in moral dilemmas (Hayakawa et al., 2017; Costa et al. 2014b; Corey et al., 2017).

In this project, we investigate whether and how the use of a foreign language shapes peoples' willingness to cooperate with others. Economic experiments have tremendously improved our understanding of human cooperation and the conditions under which people are willing to cooperate (see, e.g., Ledyard, 1995 or Zelmer, 2003 for surveys). The classical approach is the study of social dilemmas, with either public goods games or prisoner's dilemma games. In both games, individuals have to decide whether/how much to cooperate in order to reach a socially optimal outcome, yet at their own expense. We follow this approach and make use of an incentivized experiment in three languages. Subjects play a one-shot continuous prisoner's dilemma (Wahl and Novak, 1999; Dorrough and Glöckner, 2016), randomly assigned to process the experiment in either their mother tongue

S. Nothelfer, *Behavior in Foreign Languages*, Innovation und Entrepreneurship,
https://doi.org/10.1007/978-3-658-31853-6_4

or in a foreign language. We observe the behavior of 430 bilingual participants in France, Germany, and the United States across seven different combinations of mother tongue and processing language. Our experimental design not only allows us to provide causal evidence of differences in cooperation between processing in a foreign language and in the mother tongue. The study of language pairings also improves our understanding of underlying mechanisms that may lead to differences in cooperation.

Existing literature that directly relates foreign language use to cooperation is scarce and provides limited insights. Akkermans et al. (2010) find negative effects of foreign language processing on cooperation in prisoner's dilemma in a sample of Dutch native speakers when comparing processing in Dutch to processing in English. Again in a Dutch sample with Dutch/English processing, Urbig et al. (2016) study cooperation in public goods games and find a higher propensity to freeride in English than in Dutch, but no differences in overall contributions. Gargalianou et al. (2017) randomly assign Dutch business students to process the experiment in either Dutch, French, or English. In their prisoner's dilemma experiment, female participants cooperate significantly more in both foreign language treatments than in Dutch, while men tend to cooperate significantly less in foreign languages. In a Chinese sample from Hong Kong with processing in either Chinese (stronger language) or English (weaker language), subjects tend to cooperate less when playing a prisoner's dilemma in English, but no treatment differences occur in a public goods game (Li, 2017).

Some studies claim consistency with a specific type of language-related effects, such as cultural accommodation effects (Akkermans et al. 2010), or general foreign language effects, that are independent of the specific language (Urbig et al., 2016). However, without comparisons across language pairings, one cannot differentiate between language-specific effects and foreign language effects (see Chapter 2). The majority of studies rely solely on English as a foreign language. Gargalioanou et al. (2017) can at least provide a more nuanced picture across three languages in one language sample. Yet, the paper has other methodological shortcomings such as non-incentivation and a fictitious opponent in a prisoner's dilemma.

Following a more rigorous methodological approach, our paper provides novel insights into language-related effects on cooperation. With data from four different mother tongue vs. foreign language comparisons, we can clearly distinguish between a general foreign language effect and language-specific effects.

We find no indication for a general foreign language effect on cooperation, but do find evidence for language-specific effects: Participants of German mother tongue who process the experiment in French are more cooperative, compared to processing in German. Furthermore, our data show a tendency towards a positive effect of processing in German for participants of French mother tongue, that is contingent on abroad experience. Yet, effects for German-English comparisons are mostly negligible in size and insignificant, which speaks against a general foreign language effect. Our results cannot be explained with theories of cultural accommodation or ethnic affirmation either.

Furthermore, we find that abroad experience (i.e., having lived in a country where the foreign language is spoken) tends to moderate language-induced effects on cooperation. By studying the whole sample, we can show a positive effect of foreign language processing on cooperation for participants with abroad experience. This effect is absent for participants with no abroad experience and predominantly driven by the French-German language pairing.

An analysis of expectations towards the cooperation of the other player provides insights into underlying mechanisms. Based on our data, we find that processing in a foreign language tends to increase the expected cooperation of the other player. Furthermore, abroad experience has a moderating effect on expectations for participants of French and English mother tongue, and no effect on participants of German mother tongue. As the language-induced patterns of cooperation and expected cooperation are not fully congruent, our findings cannot be explained by changes in expectations with corresponding conditional cooperation.

Our results challenge the leading explanations of foreign language effects and may furthermore serve as a note of caution for future research: Results from studies in single, unidirectional combinations of mother tongue and foreign language are often difficult to interpret. In themselves, they form a weak basis for the discussion of foreign language effects.

The paper starts with a theoretical derivation of possible foreign language effects, before potentially overlapping effects and previous empirical research are discussed. We then introduce the corresponding experiment with detailed descriptions of task, subject pool, procedures, and some descriptive statistics. Our main analysis investigates patterns of cooperation and expectations towards the cooperation of others. Results are aggregated and discussed, before we conclude with limitations and an outlook for future research.

4.2 Theory

The following paragraphs summarize theory of cooperation and foreign language effects. Four potential mechanisms behind foreign language effects are discussed and theoretically linked to the field of cooperation. Based on these connections, we derive a hypothesis of a foreign language effect on cooperation. We then introduce theories of language-specific effects that may affect behavior in addition to a general foreign language effect. The theory part concludes with a critical discussion of several existing empirical studies that connect foreign language use to social dilemmas.

4.2.1 Cooperation

Human cooperation in social dilemmas has been studied extensively (see, e.g., surveys of the public goods literature in Ledyard, 1995; Zelmer, 2003; Gächter and Herrmann, 2009; and Chaudhuri, 2011). In social dilemmas, individual decisions that maximize individual monetary benefit lead to an overall sub-optimal social outcome of the group. In other words, game-theoretic Nash-equilibriums are not socially efficient. Typical games that are used to study cooperation in social dilemmas are the prisoner's dilemma, or public goods games. While standard economic theory predicts an absence of cooperation in these games, empirical evidence shows that in reality, many people do cooperate. Some people's behavior is in line with standard economic theory of non-cooperation in social dilemmas, but a large share of tested people can be described as conditional cooperators (Fischbacher, Fehr, & Gächter, 2001). Conditional cooperators increase their individual cooperation with the cooperation or the expected cooperation of others (see, e.g., Fischbacher & Gächter, 2010; Fischbacher et al., 2001; Kocher et al., 2008).

Several theories potentially explain prosocial behavior and cooperation in social dilemmas. On a general level, individual utility is likely determined not only by monetary benefits, but also by social preferences. These include intention-based fairness and reciprocity (e.g., Rabin, 1993, Dufwenberg and Kirchsteiger, 2004), payoff-based inequality aversion (e.g., Fehr and Schmidt, 1999, Bolton and Ockenfels, 2000), or forms of altruism. With his theory of warm-glow giving, Andreoni (1990) explains cooperative behavior with utility being derived directly from the act of giving, independent from the cooperative behavior of others. Furthermore, conformity with social and moral norms is a possible explanation of prosocial behavior (Krupka & Weber, 2013; Fehr & Fischbacher, 2004). Other researchers stress the importance of social emotions, such as guilt, for cooperation (Bowles & Gintis, 2002; Dufwenberg, Gächter, & Henning-Schmidt, 2010).

4.2.2 Language-Induced Effects on Behavior

Several theories predict language-induced effects on human behavior. A detailed discussion and comparison is provided in (Chapter 2). One can distinguish between language-specific effects on the one hand, and general foreign language effects on the other hand. Language-specific effects depend on the specific foreign processing language, and potentially on the mother tongue. Foreign language effects are independent of the specific processing language. They are merely caused by the fact that a processing language is foreign, i.e., different from one's mother tongue. In our study, a special emphasis lies on foreign language effects on cooperation. However, both language-specific and foreign language effects may be in place simultaneously, potentially adding up or canceling each other out. Accordingly, our empirical setup accounts for both types of effects and allows to differentiate between them.

In the following paragraphs, we first review recent research on foreign language effects and summarize findings. Potential mechanisms that cause foreign language effects are then linked to social dilemmas to derive our hypothesis of a foreign language effect on cooperation. Moreover, we present theories of language-specific effects that are relevant for our experimental design.

4.2.2.1 Foreign Language Effects

Foreign language effects that are independent of the language or one's mother tongue have been reported to affect individual preferences and shape decisions in moral dilemmas. In social dilemmas, research on foreign language effects on cooperation is relatively scarce and often has methodological shortcomings. The following paragraphs provide a summary of relevant empirical findings.

In the context of individual preferences, foreign language use has been observed to reduce decision biases such as loss aversion (Keysar, Hayakawa, & An, 2012), risk aversion, and ambiguity aversion (Costa et al. 2014a). While no effect was observed investigating the Allais paradox, foreign language processing seems to reduce inconsistent choices in tests of the Ellsberg paradox (Costa et al. 2014a). Against their initial expectation, van Hugten and van Witteloostuijn (2018) observe an increase in self-serving bias[1] for high school students of Dutch mother tongue who in English, which speaks against a general de-biasing effect of foreign language use.

[1] Self-serving bias describes the phenomenon, that individuals attribute positive outcomes to themselves (internal factors), while negative outcomes are attributed to external factors.

In moral dilemmas, processing in a foreign language has been reported to lead to a more utilitarian behavior (Costa et al. 2014b; Corey et al., 2017; Hayakawa et al., 2017; Cipolletti, McFarlane, & Weissglass, 2016). Judgments of morally questionable situations have been reported to be less severe in foreign language processing, and confidence in those judgments appears to be lower (Geipel, Hadjichristidis, & Surian, 2015).

In social dilemmas, foreign language use has been reported to increase free riding in public goods games (Urbig et al., 2016), and affect cooperation in prisoner's dilemma games (Gargalianou et al., 2017). Due to methodological shortcomings, results from the latter two studies should be interpreted with caution. The studies are discussed in more detail at the end of the theory section.

4.2.2.2 Mechanisms

Potential mechanisms behind foreign language effects are subject to debate. Emotional resonance, intuitive type 1 processing, and the salience of norms appear to be negatively influenced by foreign language processing and might drive the effects[2]. Furthermore, we discuss a potential influence of social inferences. Each of these mechanisms can by itself be linked to cooperation, which allows us to derive a working hypothesis of a negative foreign language effect on cooperation.

Reduced Type 1 Processing

The most prominent explanation of foreign language effects is related to the dual processing theory of cognition (e.g., Kahneman, 2003). Processing in a foreign language is believed to induce a shift from intuitive, fast type 1 processing, towards deliberate, slower type 2 processing (Costa et al., 2014b; Cipolletti et al., 2016; Urbig et al., 2016).

Studying moral decision making, Hayakawa et al. (2017) report that processing in a foreign language reduces type 1 processing, without improving type 2 processing. Rather than increasing deliberate thinking, processing in a foreign language might only blunt intuition.

Reviewing studies from behavioral sciences, neuroscience, and developmental psychology, Zaki and Mitchell (2013) conclude that prosocial behavior such as cooperation is often intuitive and the consequence of type 1 cognitive processing. In a series of prisoner's dilemma and public goods games, Rand, Greene, and Nowak (2012) link cooperation to the dual-process framework of cognition. By

[2]The possible mechanisms behind foreign language effects appear interrelated and not mutually exclusive—it seems possible that they refer to one and the same phenomenon (discussed in detail in Nothelfer, 2017).

analyzing response times and conducting experiments with primes that promote either intuitive or deliberate processing, they report a higher degree of cooperation for intuitive type 1 processing, and a more competitive, selfish behavior for type 2 deliberate processing[3]. A positive relationship between intuitive processing and cooperation is theoretically supported by Bear and Rand (2015), who introduce an evolutionary model of repeated prisoner's dilemmas that predicts intuitive cooperation and deliberate defection for one-shot prisoner's dilemmas.

Considering that processing in a foreign language appears to dampen intuition, i.e., seems to negatively affect type 1 processing, the level of intuitive processing may serve as a mechanism for a foreign language effect on cooperation. The direction of such an effect should be negative, i.e., the use of a foreign language would result in less cooperative behavior.

Reduction of Emotional Resonance

A significant body of studies indicate that foreign language processing appears to reduce emotional resonance (Pavlenko, 2005; Bond & Lai, 1986; Dewaele, 2004; 2010; Harris, Aycicegi, & Gleason, 2003), although this effect may be limited to negative emotions only (Wu & Thierry, 2012; Hadjichristidis, Geipel, & Savadori, 2015). Reduced emotional resonance is also widely discussed as a possible mechanism behind foreign language effects (see, e.g., Costa et al., 2014b; Cipolletti et al., 2016; Geipel, Hadjichristidis, & Surian, 2015).

Bowles and Gintis (2002) stress the importance of social emotions for prosocial behavior. In agent-based simulations of public goods games, guilt and shame are shown to steer behavior towards cooperation. Empirical evidence for increased cooperation through guilt has been provided by Ketelaar and Au (2003), Dufwenberg, Gächter, and Henning-Schmidt (2010), as well as by De Hooge, Zeelenberg, and Breugelsmans (2007).

Processing in a foreign language is likely to reduce emotional resonance. Accordingly, negative social emotions such as shame should not be as strong when processing in a foreign language. Assuming that social emotions promote cooperative behavior, one would expect a decrease in cooperation in foreign language processing, due to reduced emotional resonance.

Limited Access to Memory/ Norms

Retrieval of memory appears to be language-specific and facilitated for congruent language settings, i.e., in which the processing language during storage is identical

---

[3]Results from Rand, Greene, and Nowak (2012) are subject to a discussion, after several failed replication attempts (see e.g., Tinghög et al., 2013; Bouwmeester et al., 2017).

to the processing language during retrieval (Bartolotti & Marian, 2013; Marian & Neisser, 2000; Schrauf & Rubin, 1998; 2000). Geipel, Hadjichristidis, and Surian (2015) explain their findings on moral judgments with reduced activation of social and moral norms, which are assumed to be memorized in one's mother tongue and therefore more easily retrieved in mother-tongue processing.

In social dilemmas evolving around cooperation, moral and social norms promote cooperative behavior (Fehr & Fischbacher, 2004). Investigating moral judgments of hypothetical simultaneous and sequential two-player public goods games, Cubitt, Drouvelis, Gächter, and Kabalin (2010) report that non-cooperation is perceived as morally blameworthy in all cases, except when it reciprocates the other player's non-cooperative behavior.

Krupka and Weber (2013) have elicited social norms with incentivized judgments of dictator games. The norms promote equal sharing in dictator games and condemn scenarios in which dictators maximize their own gain. By introducing the social norms to a utility framework, the authors can predict typical behavior in dictator games, demonstrating a likely influence of social norms on behavior.

Should foreign language processing reduce the salience of social and moral norms, this would likely result in a lower level of cooperation.

Social Inferences

In the context of moral dilemmas, Corey et al. (2017) discuss social inferences in native and foreign language settings as a potential cause for more utilitarian behavior in foreign language processing. It is considered that using a foreign language may increase social distance. In the discussed trolley dilemmas, this may result in a perception of potential victims as in-group in mother tongue settings, and as out-group in foreign language settings. While Corey et al. (2017) find no empirical support for social distance as a cause for foreign language effects in moral dilemmas, social inferences may influence cooperation in social dilemmas.

In-group favoritism may be influenced by the linguistic context, potentially causing a foreign language effect. Cooperation has been observed to be larger when the other player is from the same social group, compared to other groups (Fiedler, Hellmann, Dorrough, & Glöckner, 2018; Dorrough & Glöckner, 2016; Balliet, Wu, & DeDreu, 2014; Bernhard, Fehr, & Fischbacher, 2006). Furthermore, in-group favoritism seems closely related to the concept of social distance, i.e. "the sense of coupling" (Hoffman, McCabe, & Smith, 1996) between the players. Increased social distance has a negative effect on prosocial behavior (Hoffman et al., 1996).

Based on the reported influences of social distance and in-group favoritism on cooperation, we can construct several possible relationships between foreign language processing and cooperative behavior:

First, processing in a foreign language may increase social distance, possibly through dampened emotional resonance or limited communication due to imperfect proficiency. An increase in social distance should result in decreased cooperation, indicating a possible negative effect of foreign language processing.

Second, foreign language processing may affect cooperation through different levels of in-group favoritism. Language and ethnicity are important determinants of social groups (Bernhard et al. 2006). Intuitively, we can think of two opposing effects: Processing in a foreign language might lead to increased salience of one's own (linguistic) social group (increasing in-group favoritism), or it could weaken one's own identity with the (linguistic) social group (decreasing in-group favoritism). Effects in both directions would be moderated by the in-group or out-group identity of the other player(s) in social dilemmas. An increased salience of one's own social group is theoretically similar to the theory of ethnic affirmation (see *language-specific effects*) but would result in a general foreign language effect that is independent of cultural differences.

These theoretical links between foreign language processing and cooperation via social inferences are more speculative, compared to the other theoretical links, and have a weaker empirical basis. Nevertheless, social inferences provide an additional or alternative mechanism to consider.

4.2.2.3 Hypothesis

Except for some particular cases of social inferences, all presumed mechanisms behind foreign language effects predict a negative influence on cooperation. Accordingly, we derive the following working hypothesis for our empirical investigation:

> *Foreign language processing leads to a decrease in cooperative behavior, compared to processing in the mother tongue.*

Apart from the presumed foreign language effect, foreign language use may induce overlapping language-specific effects. We must, therefore, account for language-specific effects in our experimental design. The following paragraph gives a brief overview of theories that predict potential language-specific effects on cooperation.

4.2.2.4 Language-Specific Effects

Language-specific effects can rely on characteristics of languages themselves or on constructs associated with particular languages, such as cultures or national stereotypes. Potential language-specific effects that affect cooperative behavior could be caused by cultural accommodation, linguistic relativity, ethnic affirmation, or cultural stereotypes.

Cultural accommodation requires cultural differences across groups of different mother tongues, such as nations. It predicts that individuals, who process in a foreign language, accommodate their behavior to the culture associated with that particular foreign language (Harzing & Maznevski, 2002; Akkermans, Harzing, & Van Witteloostuijn, 2010; Bond & Yang, 1982; Marian & Kaushanskaya, 2004). Behavior in a foreign language context is therefore assumed to converge towards the typical behavior of the corresponding culture.

The concept of *linguistic relativity* assumes that lexica and language structure influence thought and behavior through particular conceptualizations of time, color, space, shapes, etc. (Kay & Kempton, 1984; Boroditsky, 2001; 2003; Everett, 2013; Chen, 2013; Sutter, Angerer, Rützler, & Lergetporer, 2015). Under the assumption that different languages stand for different cultures, linguistic relativity should trigger cultural accommodation in contexts of foreign language processing (see also Chapter 2).

Ethnic affirmation is the direct opposite of cultural accommodation and also relies on cultural differences. It assumes that processing in a foreign language increases the salience of one's own culture, ultimately resulting in a behavior that is more typical of one's own culture (Yang & Bond, 1980; Bond & Yang, 1982).

Cross-country research on cooperation has revealed that *cultural stereotypes* can determine levels of cooperation. Conducting continuous Prisoner's Dilemmas in six countries, Dorrough and Glöckner (2016) identify national stereotypes as a driver for contributions. Interestingly, the observed stereotypes were mostly incorrect (i.e., negatively correlated with reality). When we adopt these findings to a cross-linguistic context, foreign language use might trigger stereotypes of the culture associated with the foreign language and thus influence behavior. Compared to cultural accommodation or ethnic affirmation, cultural stereotypes could affect behavior independently of the actual "typical" behavior of cultures and go in any direction.

4.2.3 Empirical Studies on Foreign Language Use in Social Dilemmas

The body of literature that addresses foreign language processing in social dilemmas is relatively scarce. We are familiar with four experimental studies that are methodically similar but embedded in different theoretical contexts.

To our knowledge, the only empirical study focusing on a general foreign language effect on cooperation has been conducted by Urbig et al. (2016). In public goods games with Dutch students who process in either Dutch or English, the researchers observe that students who process in English are more inclined to freeride than students who process in their Dutch mother tongue. Conscientiousness, which the researchers interpret as a predisposition for deliberate thinking, plays a moderating role: the effect is attenuated for participants with a higher level of conscientiousness. Furthermore, the processing language does not appear to affect the level of contribution for participants that decide not to freeride.

Li (2017) tested the role of language in a series of ten experiments related to social preferences. Subjects were bilinguals from Hong Kong with Chinese as their stronger language and English as their second language. The linguistic context is interpreted as a cultural prime. Li (2017) tests a general version of cultural accommodation, which he refers to as "cognitive accessibility hypothesis", against an "expectation-based hypothesis", that, similarly to cultural stereotypes, explains potential language effects with different expectations towards the behavior of others. Results contradict cultural accommodation and provide mixed evidence for the expectation-based hypothesis. Findings suggest that participants are more trusting and more trustworthy in trust games when processing in Chinese. In a simultaneous prisoner's dilemma game, participants cooperate more often on a marginal level of significance when processing in Chinese. In public goods games, Li (2017) observes no language-induced effects on cooperative behavior. Likewise, no effect of foreign language use on social preferences is observed in individual decisions without social interactions.

Akkermans, Harzing, and Van Witteloostuijn (2010) investigated the cultural accommodation hypotheses in a series of prisoner's dilemmas. Participants of Dutch mother tongue processed in either Dutch or English. The researchers report a negative effect of processing in English on cooperation, and an overall negative effect of having lived in an English-speaking country. Interactions between abroad experience and English language processing reveal that abroad experience serves as an important moderator: The negative effect of processing in English is significantly stronger for participants with abroad experience. Having lived in an English-speaking country seems to not affect participants who process in their mother tongue. While age and proficiency seemingly do not influence cooperative behavior, gender does. Female participants overall cooperated significantly less than males, but significantly more in the first shot of the prisoner's dilemma. The authors interpret their findings of language-related effects as support for cultural accommodation and do not consider the possibility of a general foreign language effect.

Similarly, Gargalianou, Urbig, & Van Witteloostuijn (2017) investigated the cultural accommodation hypothesis in a series of prisoner's dilemma games with participants of Dutch mother tongue, processing in either Dutch, French, or English. While they find no evidenee for cultural accommodation, their results suggest a language-induced effect on cooperation that is moderated by gender: Females who process in English or French are reported to cooperate more, compared to processing in Dutch. The effect is inverted for males. Results are interpreted as general foreign language effects by the authors.

Comparisons across the four studies lead to mixed results. While some findings seem in line with our hypothesis of a negative foreign language effect on cooperation, others are not. Perhaps more importantly, all four empirical studies share the methodological shortcoming of relying on data with only one mother tongue and only one or two foreign languages. In empirical setups that do not allow for pairwise comparisons across languages, one cannot distinguish between language-specific effects and foreign language effects (see Chapter 2). Also, the vast majority of subjects are of Dutch mother tongue, and the vast majority of foreign-language processing has been conducted in English. Language-specific effects of Dutch or English, possibly unrelated to cultural accommodation or ethnic affirmation, may have been in place. Overall, we consider the evidence for possible foreign language effects on cooperation to be insufficient to draw any definite conclusions.

4.3 Experimental Design

In order to test the effects of foreign language use on cooperation, we conducted a continuous prisoner's dilemma experiment (Wahl & Nowak, 1999; Dorrough & Glöckner, 2016) in three countries and three languages, cross-pairing treatment and control languages.

4.3.1 Task

Prior to starting the prisoner's dilemma, all participants received a text reproduction task. The task served as a prime, intending to trigger cognitive processing in the respective treatment language (mother tongue or foreign language). Participants were instructed to write out a short given text on a piece of paper. The text was selected to be emotion-neutral and fully comprehensible for the given threshold of minimum foreign language proficiency. After writing out the text, participants received a comprehension question on the context of the text.

The subsequent prisoner's dilemma was played anonymously as a one-shot game without communication. Participants were randomly matched to a second player of the same university with an identical decision structure. Each player received an initial endowment of 300 points. Points corresponded to monetary payoffs of one cent per point (€ in France and Germany, $ in the U.S.). Participants simultaneously had the choice between either keeping the points or transferring an amount of points t (in multiples of 30 points) to the other player. Every point transferred was doubled for the other player, i.e., the other player received twice the amount of points that the player had decided to transfer. Thus, the payoff functions for players i and j were as follows:

$$\pi_i = (300 - t_i) + 2t_j$$

$$\pi_j = \left(300 - t_j\right) + 2t_i$$

Before proceeding to the decision of how many points to transfer, control questions were asked and resolved to ensure a correct understanding of the task structure. Furthermore, participants were able to re-read the instructions and, if needed, clarify their understanding with the experimenter. Participants decided on the transfer amount, before their belief of how many points the other player would transfer was queried. Belief precision was incentivized. Detailed instructions are provided in the English version in Appendix A.3.

The Nash-equilibrium of this task lies at $t_i = t_j = 0$. Thus, standard-economic theory predicts no cooperation. However, the most surplus would be created if both players cooperated fully, transferring their entire endowments to the other player (social optimum at $t_i = t_j = 300$).

4.3.2 Factorial Design

Applying a between-subjects design, participants processed the tasks either in their mother tongue (control), or a foreign language (treatment). An incomplete[4] 3 × 3 factorial design with the factors mother tongue (French, German, or English) and processing language (French, German, or English) allows us to disentangle language-specific effects from a general foreign language effect (see Chapter 2).

Each session was equally split into treatment and control. Participants were randomly assigned to process in either their mother tongue or a foreign language. For example, German students of English processed the task in either English (treatment) or German (control), while American students of German processed the same task in either English (control) or German (treatment). The assignment to specific processing languages is random only within pairings of languages, as a fully random assignment to specific languages would require trilingual participants. However, the assignment to process in either mother tongue or foreign language is fully random across the entire sample. Since our focus lies on foreign language effects rather than on language-specific effects, we can take advantage of this full randomization. Table 4.1 provides an overview of the experimental cells.

Table 4.1 Factorial design and number of participants

Mother Tongue ▷ *Processing in* ▽	**French**	**German**	**English**	Total
French	44*	54	-	98
German	39	107*	64	210
English	-	58	64*	122
Total	83	219	128	**430**

* Control, mother tongue

_ Treatment, foreign language

The prisoner's dilemma game was part of a series of three different experiments, each with a preceding text reproduction task for language priming. The assigned processing language remained constant throughout all tasks. In order to be able to control for order-specific effects, the task order was varied in a latin-square permutation across the sessions.

[4]A complete three-by-three factorial design may prove even more informative, but would bring little methodological advantage (see Chapter 2).

4.3.3 Subject Pool

Subjects were recruited from university language programs in order to ensure foreign language proficiency and comparability across locations. The minimum foreign language proficiency level was CEFR B2[5], which should ensure a full understanding of the given instructions. In total, 469 students from seven universities in France, Germany, and the United States participated in the experiment. 39 participants with mother tongue structures that prevented a random assignment to treatment or control were excluded from analysis. These excluded participants had either both or none of the two session languages as mother tongue. The analyzed dataset was therefore drawn from 430 participants of French, German, or English mother tongue. A detailed overview of participants is provided in Appendix B.1.

4.3.4 Procedures

Participants were recruited on a voluntary basis at seven universities. Potential participants were informed that participating would not affect their studies or grades in any way.

The experimental session took place in seminar rooms or classrooms. A specifically designed mobile laboratory ensured comparable environmental conditions across all locations. The laboratory consists of testing dividers with seat numbers, experiment-specific material, modified tablet devices for instructions and inputs, and an own client-server infrastructure with Daphne and Apache servers running in a closed network (see Appendix D for details). Experimental tasks were programmed as apps using the open-source experimental platform oTree (Chen, Schonger, & Wickens, 2014) and standard web-development tools (Django, Bootstrap, Ajax). All materials were given in either the foreign treatment language or the participant's mother tongue. In order to ensure consistency across languages, all materials were translated from German and back-translated (Brislin, 1970).

Half of the seats in the laboratory were prepared for the treatment group and half for the control group. Seats and testing dividers were arranged in a way that participants could not spot any material in a different language of their own seat. A bilingual experimenter was present and answered arising questions privately in the respective processing language. Participants randomly drew seat numbers from a lottery before entering the room and were not aware of the treatment.

---

[5]B2 is an upper intermediate level in the common European framework of reference for language (CEFR).

All participants received a show-up fee of 6 €/$ in cash immediately after completion, and additional variable payments from incentivized tasks later on in cash or via bank transfer. Money was converted to points during the experiment, with a conversion rate of 1 €/$ for 100 points.

4.4 Dataset and Balance Checks

Table 4.2 shows characteristics of subject groups by treatment and by mother tongue. *Proficiency in fl* refers to self-rated proficiency in the foreign treatment language from very low (1) to very high (5). *Abroad experience fl* is a dichotomous variable with the value one if a participant has spent more than a month abroad in a country where the foreign treatment language is the main language of communication, and 0 otherwise. *Trust 1–3*, as well as *altruism 1–3* and *willingness to take risk* are survey items originally used in the German Socio-Economic Panel[6] to elicit trust, altruism, and risk. *Trust_std, altruism_std,* and *risk_std* are standardized sums of the corresponding variables that take into account different scales (see Appendix C.2 for details).

Table 4.2 Descriptive statistics of subject pools by treatment and mother tongue

	Total		Foreign language		Mother tongue		German MT		French MT		English MT	
Participants	430		215		215		219		84†		128†	
	mean	*sd*	*mean*	*sd*	*mean*	*sd*	*mean*	*sd*	*mean*	*sd*	*mean*	*sd*
Age	22.80	5.97	22.49	5.33	23.1	6.54	22.86	5.15	23.54	8.15	22.16	5.54
Female	0.65	0.48	0.66	0.48	0.64	0.48	0.73	0.45	0.65	0.48	0.52***	0.50
Proficiency in fl	4.13	0.92	4.13	0.86	4.13	0.98	4.32	0.92	4.12*	0.84	3.81***	0.88
Abroad experience in fl	0.63	0.48	0.63	0.48	0.64	0.48	0.62	0.49	0.75**	0.44	0.59	0.49
Trust 1	2.79	0.63	2.81	0.66	2.78	0.60	2.76	0.62	2.71	0.77	2.90**	0.53
Trust 2	2.97	0.74	3.00	0.78	2.93	0.69	2.96	0.69	3.04	0.83	2.95	0.76
Trust 3	2.18	0.89	2.23	0.91	2.13	0.87	2.01	0.77	2.95***	0.94	1.82***	0.74
trust_std	0.00	1.00	0.06	1.09	-0.06	0.90	-0.08	0.95	0.46***	1.13	-0.17	0.90
Altruism 1	5.35	1.23	5.44	1.19	5.27	1.26	5.35	1.17	5.37	1.52	5.35	1.11
Altruism 2	1.83	0.83	1.82	0.86	1.83	0.80	1.79	0.79	2.13***	0.93	1.70	0.80
Altruism 3	1.52	0.71	1.51	0.70	1.53	0.73	1.49	0.67	1.38	0.62	1.66**	0.81
altruism_std	0.00	1.00	0.04	0.97	-0.04	1.03	-0.01	0.90	0.28**	1.12	-0.18	1.04
Willingness to take risk	5.23	2.58	5.19	2.66	5.27	2.50	4.77	2.59	5.67***	2.53	5.73***	2.46
risk_std	0.00	1.00	-0.02	1.03	0.02	0.97	-0.18	1.00	0.17***	0.98	0.20***	0.95

All differences between Foreign language / Mother tongue are statistically insignificant (t-test). Stars indicate differences between groups of French and English mother tongues compared to German mother tongue (t-test). *** $p<0.01$, ** $p<0.05$, * $p<0.1$

† including one participant with both French and English mother tongue

[6] For an attribution of the questions to specific waves of the German Socio-Economic Panel see Becker, Deckers, Dohmen, Falk, and Kosse (2012).

The absence of significant differences between foreign language (treatment) and mother tongue (control) indicate that the randomization was successful. Systematic differences exist across subject pools of different mother tongue. While these differences should not affect our main analysis, which relies on the randomization, subject pool differences across mother tongues should be kept in mind when making cross-cultural comparisons.

4.5 Empirical Results

Our investigation begins with an analysis of transfers to directly assess cooperative behavior. We then analogously analyze expectations in order to derive insights on potential underlying mechanisms for cooperative behavior.

4.5.1 Analysis of Transfers

A first impression of the data is provided with graphical overviews of transfers by subject groups and histograms of transfer distributions. The econometric model is introduced before we present results of the regression analyses.

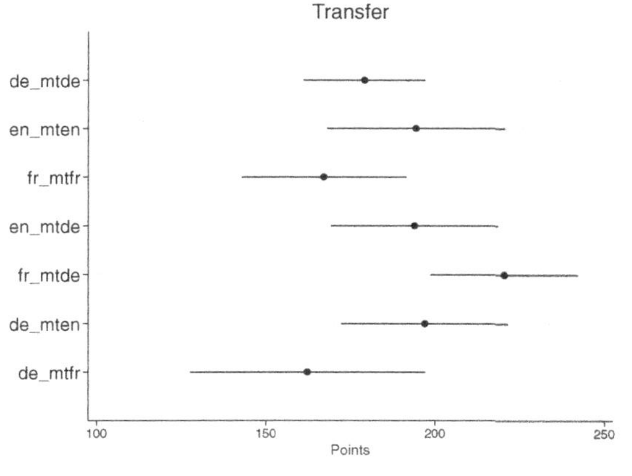

Figure 4.1 OLS estimates for transfers with mean and 95% confidence intervals by combinations of mother tongue and processing language

Figure 4.1 shows OLS estimates of transfers for each observed combination of mother tongue and processing language with means and 95% confidence intervals. The first two letters of the group names indicate the processing language (*de* for German, *fr* for French, *en* for English), while the last four letters indicate the mother tongue. For example, "en_mtde" refers to participants of German mother tongue who processed the experiment in English. The first overview shows that, on average, participants transferred a large share of their endowment to the other player, clearly demonstrating cooperation. Across the different groups, mean transfers range from about 160 points to about 220 points, from a theoretical maximum of 300 points. On this aggregate level, effects of foreign language processing seem rather weak, with one exception: Participants of German mother tongue who process in French on average seem to transfer far more than participants of German mother tongue who process in German (*fr_mtde, de_mtde* in Figure 4.1).

A graphical overview of distributions of transfers by processing in either a foreign language or mother tongue (Figure 4.2) reveals two distinct peaks. When processing in their mother tongue, about 28% of the participants transferred 150 points, which corresponds to exactly one half of the available points. This share drops to around 20% when processing in a foreign language. About 31% of the participants who played the game in their mother tongue transferred their entire endowment to the other player. This share is even higher for participants processing in a foreign language (ca. 35%). Somewhat surprisingly, shares of participants who transferred nothing are rather low in both mother tongue and foreign language processing (ca. 4% and 8%, respectively).

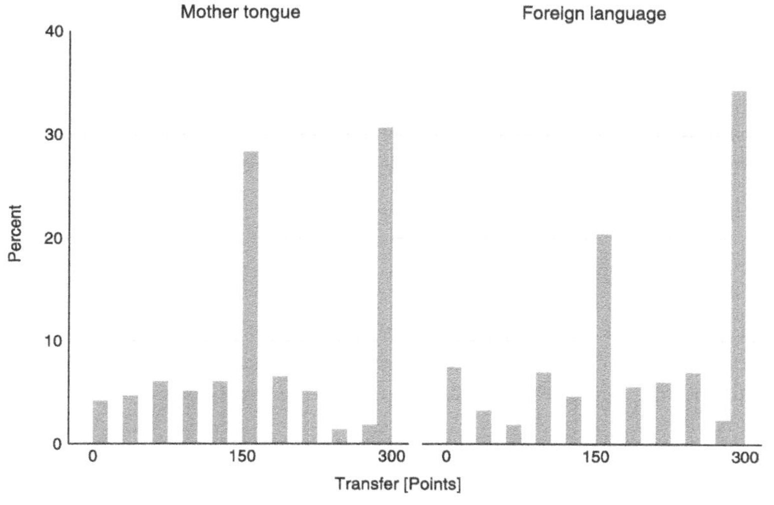

Figure 4.2 Histograms of transfers by treatment and control

Our main analysis for investigating the effect of foreign language processing on cooperation relies on OLS regressions. The dependent variable is the amount of points that a participant decided to transfer to the other player. Independent variables for languages in the models are dummies for foreign language processing (*fl*), for mother tongues French and English (*mtfr* and *mten*), interactions for processing in a foreign language and specific mother tongues (*fl*mtfr, fl*mten*), and a dummy for processing in English for participants of German mother tongue (*en_mtde*). Since the given experimental design does not include direct comparisons of French and English, the interaction terms *fl*mtfr (and fl*mten)* describe the differential effect of processing in German for participants of French (and English) mother tongue.

We start with a simple model for overall foreign language effects (Model 1a) and add independent variables for languages stepwise to achieve higher levels of detail. Comparisons across the models allow us to investigate the effects of language in detail and differentiate between general foreign language effects and language-specific effects. The following models are used for the core analysis:

Model 1a

$$Transfer_i = \beta_0 + \beta_1 * fl_i + e_i$$

The baseline for model 1a are participants of all mother tongues, processing in their mother tongue. β_1 estimates the role of general foreign language processing.

Model 1b

$$Transfer_i = \beta_0 + \beta_1 * fl_i + \beta_2 * mten_i + \beta_3 * mtfr_i + e_i$$

The baseline for model 1b are participants of German mother tongue, processing in German. β_1 estimates the role of general foreign language processing. β_2 and β_3 estimate the influence of having English or French mother tongue, compared to the baseline.

Model 1c

$$Transfer_i = \beta_0 + \beta_1 * fl_i + \beta_2 * mten_i + \beta_3 * mtfr_i + \beta_4 * fl_i * mten_i + \beta_5 * fl_i * mtfr_i + e_i$$

The baseline for model 1c are participants of German mother tongue, processing in German. Due to added interactions between foreign language processing and English/French mother tongues, β_1 estimates the role of foreign language processing for participants of German mother tongue only. β_2 and β_3 estimate the differential effect of having English or French mother tongue for participants that process in their mother tongue, compared to the baseline. The sums $(\beta_1 + \beta_4)$ and $(\beta_1 + \beta_5)$ estimate the effect of processing in German on participants of English and French mother tongues, as the only foreign language for participants of English and French is German.

Model 1d

$$Transfer_i = \beta_0 + \beta_1 * fl_i + \beta_2 * mten_i + \beta_3 * mtfr_i + \beta_4 * fl_i * mten_i + \beta_5 * fl_i * mtfr_i + \beta_6 * en\_mtde_i + e_i$$

The baseline for model 1d are participants of German mother tongue, who process in German. Due to added interactions between foreign language processing and English/French mother tongues, and a dummy *en_mtde*, β_1 estimates the role of French processing for participants of German mother tongue only. As participants of German mother tongue could process in either French or English as foreign languages, the dummy *en_mtde* differentiates English processing from French processing and should be interpreted in the same way as the interactions *fl*mtfr, fl*mten*. β_2 and β_3 estimate the influence of having an English or French mother tongue for participants who process in their mother tongues, compared to the baseline. The sums ($\beta_1 + \beta_4$) and ($\beta_1 + \beta_5$) estimate the effect of processing in German on participants of English and French mother tongue. The sum ($\beta_1 + \beta_6$) estimates the effect of English processing for participants of German mother tongue.

Model 1e extends model 1d with additional control variables for robustness checks. Control variables include standardized indicators for being generally trusting (*trust_std*), altruistic (*altruism_std*), and willing to take risks (*risk_std*). Details on these indicators are provided in Appendix C, Table C-6. Furthermore, age, gender, proficiency, and task order are controlled for. The order variables are dummy variables with value one if this task was first/third, and 0 otherwise. Furthermore, we include a dummy for abroad experience in a country with the foreign language.

As previous research indicated potential moderating effects of abroad experience (Akkermans et al., 2010) and gender (Gargalianou et al., 2017), we investigate potential moderating effects of these two variables in additional OLS regressions (models 2a-d and 3a-d). In these models, other coefficients that include foreign language processing variables must be interpreted contingent on abroad experience/female gender.

4.5.1.1 Main Regressions

First, we analyze transfer decisions without control variables and interactions of abroad experience and gender. Results from corresponding OLS regressions (models 1a-d in Table 4.3) do not indicate a general foreign language effect on the level of cooperation (*fl* in models 1a and 1b) across all subject pools. While the corresponding coefficient (*fl* in models 1a and 1b) is positive, it is not significant and appears to be driven by participants of German mother tongue only. No effect for processing in German is observable for participants of French or English mother tongues (Wald-tests model 1d: *fl* + *fl*mtfr*, $p = 0.871$; *fl* + *fl*mten*, $p = 0.868$). When processing in French, participants of German mother tongue transfer on average 36 more points to the other player than when processing in German (significant *fl* coefficient in model 1d). For German native speakers who process in English, this effect seems absent, although the sum of the corresponding coefficients is positive (*en_mtde* + *fl*, $p = 0.736$ in model 1d). Accordingly, a language-specific effect of processing in French for participants of German mother tongue seems to be in place. Participants of French mother tongue overall transfer significantly less points to the other player than participants of German mother tongue (*mtfr* in model 1b), potentially indicating a cultural difference between participants of French and German mother tongue.

Table 4.3 OLS regressions on transfers to the other player

VARIABLES	(1a) PD Transfer	(1b) PD Transfer	(1c) PD Transfer	(1d) PD Transfer	(1e) PD Transfer
fl	11.302	10.520	20.272	36.393**	41.483***
	(9.276)	(9.282)	(12.410)	(14.254)	(14.461)
mten		2.778	11.359	11.359	18.437
		(10.899)	(15.705)	(15.724)	(15.258)
mtfr		-28.047**	-16.749	-16.749	-23.129
		(11.979)	(14.439)	(14.456)	(14.657)
fl*mten			-17.252	-33.373	-40.892*
			(21.840)	(22.955)	(22.532)
fl*mtfr			-23.711	-39.832	-47.866*
			(24.335)	(25.346)	(24.650)
en_mtde				-31.130*	-36.353**
				(16.921)	(17.326)
trust_std					3.253
					(5.358)
altruism_std					17.445***
					(4.871)
risk_std					4.084
					(4.834)
age					1.673***
					(0.646)
female					-15.392
					(9.817)
abroad experience					4.723
					(10.184)
proficiency					10.085**
					(5.061)
order: pd third					-4.506
					(11.288)
order: pd first					11.830
					(12.196)
Constant	182.372***	187.415***	182.496***	182.496***	106.735***
	(6.421)	(7.873)	(8.922)	(8.932)	(30.764)
Observations	430	430	430	430	430
R-squared	0.003	0.018	0.021	0.028	0.096

OLS. Robust standard errors in parentheses.
*** p<0.01, ** p<0.05, * p<0.1

Comparing directions of the potential cultural difference with language-specific effects, our results contradict the theory of cultural accommodation and are in line with one-sided ethnic affirmation (see Chapter 2).

Results persist when we introduce control variables (model 1e). Coefficients for altruism, trust, and the willingness to take risks suggest that transfers are at least partly motivated by altruism, while trust and risk propensity play a less important role (*altruism_std, risk_std, trust_std* in model 1e). Age appears to influence cooperation positively. Furthermore, proficiency in the foreign language has a positive effect. No significant effect of abroad experience and gender can be observed.

4.5.1.2 Moderating Effects of Abroad Experience and Gender

Table 4.4 explores previously reported moderating effects of abroad experience (Akkermans et al., 2010) and gender (Gargalianou et al., 2017). Models 2a-d extend models 1a-d with interactions between foreign language processing and abroad experience. Models 3a-d include interactions between foreign language processing and gender. Due to the added interactions, we must differentiate between participants with and without abroad experience in models 2a-d (and female and male participants in models 3a-d) when analyzing coefficients with foreign language components.

Abroad Experience

The interaction term *fl*abroad experience* is strongly positive and at the edge of marginal significance in models 2a-d, suggesting a positive moderating effect of abroad experience. In line with this positive coefficient, we observe corresponding differences between participants with and without abroad experiences.

For participants *without abroad experience*, there appears to be no overall foreign language effect (*fl* in models 2a-b). A positive, yet insignificant, effect may be in place for participants of German mother tongue without experience abroad who process in French (*fl* in model 2d, $p = 0.406$). The joint coefficients for other foreign language/mother tongue combinations for participants without abroad experience are almost zero or negative, and insignificant (Wald tests in model 2d; *fl + fl*mten,* $p = 0.455$; *fl + fl*mtfr,* $p = 0.279$; *fl + en_mtde,* $p = 0.522$). Given the potential cultural differences between French and German, negative coefficients for *fl*mtfr + fl* would be in line with ethnic affirmation and contradict the theory of cultural accommodation.

For participants *with abroad experience*, the coefficients (*fl*abroad_experience + fl*), that jointly indicate an overall foreign language effect in models 2a-b, are in sum strongly positive and significant (Wald tests, model 2a: $p = 0.046$; model

Table 4.4 OLS regressions on transfers to the other player with interactions for abroad experience and gender

VARIABLES	(2a) PD Transfer	(2b) PD Transfer	(2c) PD Transfer	(2d) PD Transfer	(3a) PD Transfer	(3b) PD Transfer	(3c) PD Transfer	(3d) PD Transfer
fl	-8.442	-9.536	0.125	15.830	-1.505	-0.837	9.397	27.488
	(15.881)	(15.661)	(17.446)	(19.019)	(16.347)	(16.244)	(19.828)	(20.248)
mten		2.469	10.983	10.983		-0.245	6.398	6.398
		(10.899)	(15.727)	(15.746)		(11.136)	(15.981)	(16.000)
mtfr		-30.037**	-16.313	-16.313		-28.539**	-17.194	-17.194
		(11.887)	(14.547)	(14.565)		(12.092)	(14.486)	(14.503)
fl*mten			-17.196	-31.946			-13.482	-30.453
			(21.848)	(22.907)			(22.342)	(23.218)
fl*mtfr			-29.051	-43.551*			-24.037	-40.868
			(24.042)	(24.966)			(24.573)	(25.451)
en_mtde				-28.517*				-32.003*
				(17.040)				(16.708)
abroad experience	-7.142	-4.290	-4.666	-4.666				
	(13.287)	(13.305)	(13.347)	(13.363)				
fl*abroad exprience	31.161	31.587	33.339*	31.772				
	(19.530)	(19.310)	(19.459)	(19.474)				
female					-23.619*	-22.447*	-21.578	-21.578
					(13.486)	(13.585)	(13.771)	(13.788)
female*fl					20.057	17.807	15.444	13.395
					(19.830)	(19.787)	(20.280)	(20.028)
Constant	186.923***	190.658***	185.490***	185.490***	197.532***	202.826***	197.917***	197.917***
	(10.511)	(11.257)	(11.965)	(11.979)	(10.965)	(12.203)	(13.299)	(13.314)
Observations	430	430	430	430	430	430	430	430
R-squared	0.011	0.027	0.031	0.037	0.011	0.024	0.027	0.034

OLS. Robust standard errors in parentheses.
*** p<0.01, ** p<0.05, * p<0.1

2b: p = 0.054). When investigating individual languages within the foreign language treatment, the previously observed positive effect of French processing for participants of German mother tongue is clearly present and of high effect size for participants with abroad experience (*fl*abroad_experience* + *fl* in model 2d, Wald test p<0.003). Joint coefficients for *fl*abroad_experience* and other foreign language treatments are positive, but insignificant (Wald tests in model 2d; *fl*abroad_experience* + *fl*mtfr* + *fl*, p = 0.847; *fl*abroad_experience* + *fl*mten* + *fl*, p = 0.429; *fl*abroad_experience* + *en*mtde* + *fl*, p = 0.274). An additional subgroup analysis of data from participants with abroad experience only (Appendix C.1.1) provides a clearer picture. No effect of English processing is observed for participants of German mother tongue. Likewise, no effect of German processing appears to be in place for participants of English mother tongue. Coefficients for participants of French mother tongue with abroad experience who process in German are positive, but not significant (*fl* + *fl*mtfr* in model 7c, Wald test p = 0.337). Accordingly, the positive, jointly significant coefficients (*fl*abroad_experience* + *fl*) in models 2a-b are driven by the German/French language pairing only. Rather than an overall foreign language effect contingent on abroad experience, we seem to observe language-specific positive effects of processing in German or French as foreign languages, which are in effect for participants of German or French mother tongue.

In order to further investigate the potential moderating effect of abroad experience, we conducted additional subgroup analyses by language combinations (Appendix C.1). A clear moderating effect exists for participants of French mother tongue who process in German (Table C-2). For participants of German mother tongue who process in French (Table C-3), as well as for English native speakers who process in German (Table C-5), the moderating effect is positive, but not significant. No moderating effect can be observed for participants of German mother tongue who process in English (Table C-4), who also show no language effect. In summary, our data show a strong tendency towards a moderating role of abroad experience for a positive foreign language effect on cooperation but lack statistical significance for stronger conclusions.

Gender

Negative coefficients for *female* in models 3a-d at the edge of significance suggest a potentially lower level of cooperation for females without abroad experience, compared to males. The interaction between female and foreign language processing *female*fl* is positive, but not significant.

For male participants, no foreign language effect can be observed (*fl* in models 3a-b). The positive, yet statistically insignificant, coefficient for *fl* in model 3d indicates a potential positive effect of processing in French for male participants of German mother tongue.

Analyzing female participants, the coefficients (*female*fl* + *fl*), which jointly indicate an overall foreign language effect for females in models 3a-b, are positive and jointly close to marginal significance (Wald test, *female*fl* + *fl*; model 3a $p = 0.010$; model 3b $p = 0.134$). However, this effect seems to be only driven by female participants of German mother tongue who process in French (*female*fl* + *fl* in model 3d, Wald test $p = 0.007$), as the other joint coefficients add up to almost zero in model 3d (*female*fl* + *fl* + *fl*mten; female*fl* + *fl* + *fl*mtfr; female*fl* + *fl* + *en_mtde*).

Accordingly, gender does not seem to be a moderator for a general foreign language effect, but females of German mother tongue appear to show a stronger language-specific effect of processing in French, compared to males of German mother tongue.

4.5.2 Analysis of Expected Transfers

Investigating expectations of the incoming transfer from the other player may provide additional information on the background of the previously observed language-induced effects. Should expectations be affected in the same way as transfers, a change in expectations may explain the language-specific effects, in line with the concept of conditional cooperation. Should language-induced changes in expectation be incongruent to language-induced changes in transferred points, this could indicate potential language-induced effects due to warm-glow or similar social preferences.

The analysis is conducted analogously to the analysis of transfers. The dependent variable in models 4–6 is the expected transfer. Independent variables are identical to models 1–3. It should be noted that, while the expected incoming transfer was incentivized, it was elicited after participants had made their transfer decision. Therefore, data on expected transfers are methodologically weaker than data on transfers.

The analysis starts with graphical overviews. Figure 4.3 shows OLS estimates for each observed combination of mother tongue and processing language with means and 95% confidence intervals.

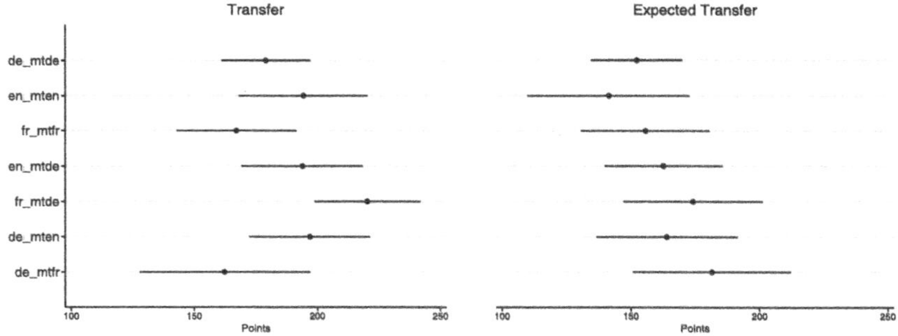

Figure 4.3 OLS estimates for transfers and expected transfers with mean and 95% confidence intervals by combinations of mother tongue and processing language

On average, participants expect the other player to cooperate. Mean expected transfers range from slightly below 150 points from participants of English mother tongue who processed in English, to about 180 points for participants of French mother tongue who processed in German. Groups who processed in a foreign language appear to expect a slightly higher degree of cooperation, compared to groups who processed in their mother tongues.

On this aggregate level, transfers and expected transfers are congruent for some groups only. Interestingly, participants of English mother tongue who processed in English or German, and participants of German mother tongue who processed in French, on average transferred more than what they expected the other player would transfer. This behavior is neither in line with standard-economic theory, nor with conditional contribution, but could indicate warm-glow giving.

A graphical overview of distributions of expected transfers by processing in either a foreign language or mother tongue (Figure 4.4) reveals three distinct peaks. When processing in their mother tongue, about 15% of the participants expect no incoming transfer at all, about 28% expect the other player to transfer half her points, and about 25% expect the other player to cooperate fully and transfer all points. In the foreign language treatment, these peaks appear to be in place as well, while the share of participants expecting 0 points is roughly 10%, and the share of participants expecting full cooperation is about 27%. Interestingly, in both language conditions, the share of participants expecting an incoming transfer of 0 is higher than the share of participants transferring nothing to the other player. This pattern indicates that some participants' behavior is likely driven by altruism or overall efficiency considerations.

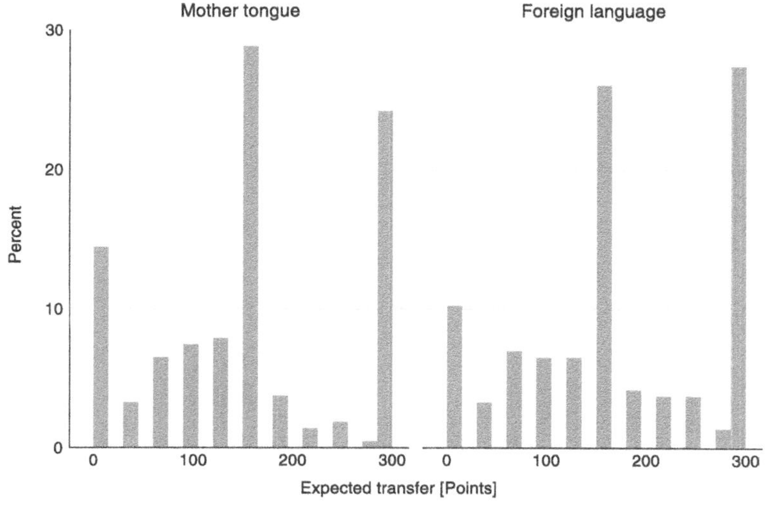

Figure 4.4 Histograms of expected transfers by treatment and control

4.5.2.1 Main Regressions

OLS regressions with the expected transfer of the other player as the dependent variable (Table 4.5) reveal a marginally significant positive effect of foreign language processing (*fl* in model 4b). This effect is of similar size for participants of English and French mother tongues who processed in German, and German participants who processed in French (model 4d: *fl*mten* + *fl*, p = 0.286; *fl*mtfr* + *fl*, p = 0.228; *fl*, p = 0.238). It seems to be absent for participants of German mother tongue who processed in English (model 4d: *fl* + *en_mtde*, p = 0.954).

Table 4.5 OLS regressions on expected point transfers from the other player

VARIABLES	(4a) Exp. Transf.	(4b) Exp. Transf.	(4c) Exp. Transf.	(4d) Exp. Transf.	(4e) Exp. Transf.
fl	16.047	16.271*	9.690	19.174	24.848
	(9.778)	(9.811)	(12.727)	(16.231)	(16.980)
mten		-8.447	-14.839	-14.839	-7.955
		(12.204)	(17.921)	(17.942)	(17.305)
mtfr		8.057	1.282	1.282	-5.312
		(11.560)	(14.810)	(14.827)	(15.530)
fl*mten			12.830	3.346	-4.629
			(24.466)	(26.478)	(25.798)
fl*mtfr			14.185	4.701	-8.753
			(23.373)	(25.469)	(25.867)
en_mtde				-18.314	-24.306
				(18.135)	(19.003)
trust_std					9.469*
					(5.275)
altruism_std					14.483***
					(5.101)
risk_std					12.474**
					(4.985)
age					1.296*
					(0.743)
female					-0.154
					(10.521)
abroad experience					-5.211
					(10.576)
proficiency					11.181**
					(5.292)
order: pd third					-10.212
					(12.127)
order: pd first					10.906
					(13.177)
Constant	152.233***	153.061***	156.382***	156.382***	83.882**
	(6.944)	(8.043)	(8.931)	(8.941)	(35.157)
Observations	430	430	430	430	430
R-squared	0.006	0.009	0.011	0.013	0.090

OLS. Robust standard errors in parentheses.
*** p<0.01, ** p<0.05, * p<0.1

When adding control variables (model 4e), the patterns remain relatively similar, indicating robustness. High levels of altruism, trust, and the willingness to take risks all seem to affect expectations positively. Also, increasing age and foreign language proficiency seem to have a positive effect.

Overall, we observe a tendency towards an increase of expected cooperation as a result of foreign language use, with the exception of processing in English for German native speakers. The previously observed pattern of cooperation is only partly mirrored in changed expectations. Accordingly, not all language-induced effects seem to be explainable by changed expectations.

4.5.2.2 Moderating Effects of Abroad Experience and Gender

Analogous to the analysis of transfers, we investigate potential moderating effects of abroad experience and gender on expected cooperation (Table 4.6).

Table 4.6 OLS regressions on expected transfers of the other player with interactions for abroad experience and gender

VARIABLES	(5a) Exp. Transf.	(5b) Exp. Transf.	(5c) Exp. Transf.	(5d) Exp. Transf.	(6a) Exp. Transf.	(6b) Exp. Transf.	(6c) Exp. Transf.	(6d) Exp. Transf.
fl	-3.539	-3.636	-9.577	-0.393	23.297	22.850	15.628	26.290
	(16.088)	(16.072)	(18.278)	(20.718)	(17.475)	(17.432)	(20.057)	(22.455)
mten		-9.061	-15.914	-15.914		-8.352	-13.866	-13.866
		(12.171)	(17.932)	(17.953)		(12.319)	(18.034)	(18.055)
mtfr		7.236	2.528	2.528		7.800	1.369	1.369
		(11.510)	(14.861)	(14.879)		(11.622)	(14.829)	(14.847)
fl*mten			13.705	5.079			11.094	1.091
			(24.406)	(26.517)			(24.714)	(26.686)
fl*mtfr			9.877	1.398			13.604	3.685
			(23.289)	(25.508)			(23.532)	(25.621)
en_mtde				-16.676				-18.862
				(18.260)				(18.108)
abroad experience	-11.586	-13.088	-13.337	-13.337				
	(14.361)	(14.438)	(14.542)	(14.559)				
fl*abroad exprience	30.878	31.338	31.240	30.324				
	(20.252)	(20.224)	(20.505)	(20.445)				
female					7.120	5.083	4.234	4.234
					(14.667)	(14.661)	(14.689)	(14.706)
female*fl					-11.178	-10.115	-8.163	-9.371
					(21.085)	(21.106)	(21.279)	(21.227)
Constant	159.615***	161.755***	164.939***	164.939***	147.662***	149.824***	153.356***	153.356***
	(11.365)	(12.000)	(12.670)	(12.685)	(11.908)	(12.607)	(13.245)	(13.261)
Observations	430	430	430	430	430	430	430	430
R-squared	0.012	0.015	0.016	0.018	0.007	0.010	0.011	0.013

OLS regression. Robust standard errors in parentheses.
*** $p<0.01$, ** $p<0.05$, * $p<0.1$

Abroad Experience

Coefficients for the interaction *fl*abroad experience* are of high effect size and positive throughout models 5a-d, but statistically not significant ($p = 0.128$ in model 5a), indicating only a tendency towards a positive moderating effect of abroad experience. This pattern is analogous to the transfers.

For participants *without* abroad experience, no effect of foreign language processing appears to be in place (*fl* in models 5a-b). In addition, no significant language-specific effect can be observed (model 5d).

For participants *with* abroad experience, we observe a positive and significant foreign language effect of moderate size on expected transfers (*fl* + *fl*abroad experience,* $p = 0.027$ in model 5a). This effect appears to be slightly less driven by participants of German mother tongue who process in English, than by the other foreign language groups, as the coefficient for *en_mtde* is negative of moderate size, while other foreign-language coefficients are almost zero (model 5d).

An additional subgroup analysis of different combinations of mother tongue and treatment language reveals that the moderating effect of abroad experience is positive and very strong for participants of French and English mother tongue, while it appears to be absent or even negative for participants of German mother tongue (Appendix C.1). While the observed moderating effects of abroad experience are not congruent between expected cooperation and cooperation, they share a common positive direction.

Gender
Coefficients for the interaction *female*fl* are small in models 6a-d and far from being significant (e.g., $p = 0.597$ in model 6a). Therefore, gender does not seem to have a moderating effect on expected cooperation.

4.6 Discussion

What is the impact of foreign language use on cooperation? This paper derives a possible foreign language effect from theory, connecting language-induced effects to social dilemmas. The effect of foreign language processing is investigated empirically with an international experiment in three languages in France, Germany, and the United States.

We rely on data from a statistically meaningful sample of 430 participants from seven universities and six different cities. Participants were randomly assigned to process the experiment in either their mother tongue or a foreign language. Tasks include a prime for the processing language and an incentivized one-shot continuous prisoner's dilemma with subsequent elicitation of expectations. To our knowledge, this is the most comprehensive study of the role of language on cooperation and the only study that can differentiate between language-specific effects and foreign language effects. Empirical results extend our knowledge about foreign language effects in the important field of cooperation and challenge previous findings. Our main findings can be summarized as follows:

Foreign Language Effect
In contrast to our hypothesis, we observe no general foreign language effect on cooperation. However, we find suggestive evidence for a moderating role of abroad experience (i.e., having lived in a country with the foreign processing language). While the positive overall coefficient for testing the moderating role of abroad experience lacks significance, subgroup analysis confirms a stable tendency. Accordingly, we should differentiate between subjects without, and subjects with abroad experience.

For participants *without* abroad experience, our data speaks against a foreign language effect.

For participants *with* abroad experience, we retrieve mixed results. Overall, participants with abroad experience cooperate significantly more when processing in a foreign language, compared to processing in their mother tongue. However, this result is driven by subjects of the French-German language pairing, which account for roughly half of our data. No language-induced effect seems to be in place in the English-German language pairing.

In conclusion, our results support positive effects of foreign language processing on cooperation in the French-German language pairing, that are contingent on abroad experience, but no overarching foreign language effect.

Expectations as Drivers
Cooperation in social dilemmas can to some degree be explained by conditional cooperation, i.e., cooperation increases with the cooperation or expected cooperation of others (see, e.g., Fischbacher & Gächter, 2010; Fischbacher, Gächter, & Fehr, 2001; Kocher et al., 2008).

We show that foreign language use tends to increase expectations on cooperation. In addition, abroad experience appears to positively moderate this effect for participants of English and French mother tongue, but not for participants of German mother tongue.

When we compare our findings of positive language-induced effects on cooperation with the findings on expectations, the two pictures are not entirely congruent. Changes in expectations are an insufficient explanation for the differences in the effects of language on cooperation, in particular between the strong effects of processing in French for participants of German mother tongue and the absence of effects of processing in German for participants of English mother tongue. In addition, transfers partly exceeded expectations, which is at odds with previously observed contribution patterns in social dilemmas and strategies of conditional cooperation (Fischbacher et al., 2001).

Accordingly, the observed language-induced effects cannot be attributed entirely to changes in expectations that result in behavior differences through conditional cooperation.

Language-Specific Effects

We observe a clear positive language-specific effect on cooperation for participants of German mother tongue who process in French. Furthermore, for participants of French mother tongue who process in German, we observe a tendency towards increased cooperation that is contingent on abroad experience.

Furthermore, our data suggest a corresponding cultural difference: Participants of French mother tongue seem to cooperate less than participants of German mother tongue. Accordingly, the language-specific effect of French processing for participants of German mother tongue directly contradicts the theory of cultural accommodation. Additionally, the tendency of a positive effect of German processing for French native speakers with abroad experience contradicts the theory of ethnic affirmation.

A possible, yet speculative explanation for the effect are cultural stereotypes that differ from the actual observed cultural differences. As the higher level of cooperation in French processing for participants of German mother tongue appears to be backed by higher expected cooperation of the other player, a positive national stereotype of French cooperation levels might be in place. However, two aspects may cast doubt on cultural stereotypes as the driving force: participants are told that the other player belongs to the same university as they do, and we have no empirical evidence suggesting that foreign language use is a sufficient prime to trigger influences of cultural stereotypes on cooperation.

Overall, the language-specific effect of French processing on participants of German mother tongue remains a phenomenon that we cannot explain to a satisfying degree. Further investigations of this effect and replication attempts with different subject pools seem advisable. Nonetheless, the existence of language-specific effects demonstrates the importance of investigating several languages in cross-parings for research on the foreign language effect.

Comparison to Previous Research

Our results stand in contrast to previous empirical findings. Akkermans et al. (2010) and Urbig et al. (2016) report negative effects of processing in English on cooperation for participants of Dutch mother tongue. We observe no negative effect of processing in English for participants of German mother tongue. Our findings contradict cultural accommodation as an explanation for language-induced effects, in particular as provided by Akkermans et al. (2010), who differentiate between Anglo-Saxon culture and Rhineland culture.

This study's findings show that processing in a foreign language can have a positive influence on cooperation for individuals with corresponding abroad experience. Also, our data demonstrate that language-specific effects can exist and should not be generalized unless proven for a more extensive variety of language combinations. While this study does not replicate previous experiments that rely mostly on Dutch and English, our results suggest that many previously reported findings are likely to be language-specific effects and no evidence for general foreign language effects or cultural accommodation.

4.7 Limitations and Outlook

As any experimental study, this study has some methodological boundaries that may affect its generalizability. Limitations are discussed in the following paragraphs and suggestions for further research are made.

Both the decision to transfer points to the other player and the elicitation of belief are incentivized. However, we elicit expectations after participants have made their own transfer decision. The preceding transfer decision may have influenced the reported expected transfers. The expected transfers are therefore methodologically weaker than the actual transfers and should be interpreted with caution. Nonetheless, we believe that there is some informative value in the expected transfers.

Our allocation of participants to process in either their mother tongue or a foreign language is fully randomized. The assignment to a specific processing language is only random within each of the two cross-pairings of languages (i.e., English/German and French/German). Hence, inferences on language-specific effects rely on smaller sample sizes than inferences on foreign language effects.

Testing seven combinations of pairings of three languages as mother tongues and foreign languages accounts only for a tiny fraction of the languages and cultures in this world. France, Germany, and the U.S. are all part of the "Western" world and may be culturally more similar to each other than to countries from Africa or Asia. French, English, and German are all Indo-Germanic languages. While our results speak against a general foreign language effect on cooperation, it would be interesting to conduct additional research with different cultures and logographic languages, such as Mandarin. Furthermore, the likely absence of a general foreign language effect does not imply that foreign language use has, in general, no influence on cooperation. Undiscovered language-specific effects are likely to affect behavior, and we know very little about their prevalence and relevance.

This study relies on comparable subject pools with different mother tongues from different countries. All our subjects are language students of universities, and they are clearly not representative of national societies. Accordingly, cooperation behavior in our subject pools may systematically differ from other groups in societies. While the generalizability of the observed cooperation behavior to entire societies remains questionable, we have no reason to believe that our subjects are influenced by foreign language processing differently than other people who process in a foreign language. After all, the group of people who regularly interact in foreign languages are most likely not representative for entire societies and may share various characteristics with our subject pools (e.g., above-average level of education; proficiency in foreign languages).

Last but not least, while our findings contradict some potential mechanisms, the driving forces behind language-specific effects remain unclear. In particular, we cannot explain the causes for the language-specific effect of French processing on participants of German mother tongue. For future research, it would be interesting to further investigate the causes for language-specific effects. Cultural accommodation, linguistic relativity, and ethnic affirmation provide unsatisfactory explanations. As we observe some language-induced effects on expectations, the relationship between cultural stereotypes and foreign language use is a promising field for further investigations. Knowledge about the mechanisms of language-specific effects may help us to assess their scope and relevance in more depth.

5 Conclusion and Outlook

To what extend does the use of a foreign language affect behavior? While much more research seems necessary to answer this fundamental question to a satisfying degree, this dissertation provides some new pieces to the puzzle.

The thesis contributes to theory about language-induced effects and extends empirical research to the important domains of human cooperation and creativity. With newly generated data from an international series of experiments, it allows for causal inferences and contributes to the empirical evidence needed for cross-disciplinary studies of language-induced effects on behavior. To my knowledge, these are the first experimental studies on language-induced effects on creativity, and cooperation that examine language pairings, which allows to differentiate between several effect types. With English, French, and German, the thesis examines languages that are frequently used by non-native speakers and highly relevant to the professional world.

Overall, no general foreign language effects on either creativity, cooperation, or cheating have been observed. Yet, foreign language use appears to yield higher self-evaluations of their own creative products for participants without living experience in a country with the foreign language. Furthermore, foreign language use may increase expectations of the cooperative behavior of others.

The absence of statistically significant foreign language effects on creativity and cooperation in our sample must not lead us to the false conclusion that foreign language use has no effect on these two domains. In fact, we demonstrate that foreign language use does systematically influence creativity and cooperative behavior for specific combinations of foreign language and mother tongue. The collected data provide evidence for several such language-specific effects: French native speakers who use German as a foreign language appear to be more

S. Nothelfer, *Behavior in Foreign Languages*, Innovation und Entrepreneurship, https://doi.org/10.1007/978-3-658-31853-6_5

creative, compared to processing in French. German native speakers who process in French cooperate more, compared to processing in German. Furthermore, we observe a tendency towards increased cooperation for French native speakers with living experience in a German-speaking country when they process in German, compared to processing in French. Similarly, we observe a tendency towards decreased cheating for German native speakers with living experience in a French-speaking country when they process in French, compared to processing in German. Patterns of individual language-specific effects contradict predictions of cultural accommodation or ethnic affirmation.

Results of this dissertation contribute to several streams of research:

The dissertation challenges the theories of cultural accommodation and ethnic affirmation (see, e.g., Earle, 1969; Bond & Yang, 1982; Church et al., 1988; Akkermans et al., 2010; Harzing & Maznevski, 2002; Gargalianou et al., 2017). Empirical results in combination with the theoretical disentanglement of potential language-induced effects suggest that most of the previously reported empirical evidence for cultural accommodation cannot rule out other language-specific effects as alternative explanations. Studies without language pairings must be interpreted with caution. Without methodologically rigorous studies that replicate previous findings, theories of cultural accommodation and ethnic affirmation lack empirical support and should not be sustained.

The experiments on creativity, cooperation, and cheating contribute to corresponding literature streams that examine environmental influences on these behavioral domains. Moreover, our cross-country data can contribute to cross-cultural research in these topics, yet with the limitation of comparable, but non-representative subject pools.

Perhaps most importantly, the dissertation contributes to the ongoing exploration of foreign language effects (see, e.g., Keysar et al., 2012; Hayakawa et al., 2017; Corey et al., 2017; Costa et al., 2014a; 2014b; Urbig et al., 2016). Results shed some light on the scope and boundaries of foreign language effects and extend the empirical research to the domains of creativity, cheating, and cooperation. While this dissertation does not address underlying cognitive mechanisms of foreign language effects, its findings may prove a valuable supplement to future research that targets underlying mechanisms of foreign language effects.

Overall, the picture is complex and nuanced, considering the language-specific effects in some behavioral domains and certain languages. Focusing on the mechanisms behind language-induced effects seems to be the best way to move forward. Without a better understanding of mechanisms, exploring language-induced effects in other domains and languages would possibly reveal other language-specific effects, but appears to be a cumbersome and inefficient approach to achieve a comprehensive picture of the role of foreign language use for behavior. A better understanding of the cognitive effects of foreign language use would allow us to make more informed theoretical predictions of language-induced effects and their boundaries. Thus, cross-disciplinary efforts from the fields of neuroscience, linguistics, psychology, and behavioral economics may eventually lead to a good understanding of the fundamental relationship between foreign language use and behavior.

Appendix A: Supplement to "In Search of Cultural Accommodation, Ethnic Affirmation, and Foreign Language Effects"

A.1 Experimental Instructions

The following screenshots show the English version of the cheating experiment. Participants start with the priming task before proceeding to the die roll. Each image corresponds to one page displayed on the tablet device. Please note that the logic behind buttons and input fields is not visible from these screenshots (Figures A-1, A-2, A-3, A-4, A-5, A-6, A-7 and A-8).

S. Nothelfer, *Behavior in Foreign Languages*, Innovation und Entrepreneurship,
https://doi.org/10.1007/978-3-658-31853-6

General Information

Welcome to this study by the Max-Planck-Institute for Innovation and Competition in Munich in cooperation with The Ohio State University.
This study has no bearing on your program of study and does not affect your grades.
All details and decisions will be analyzed confidentially. The data will be used exclusively for academic purposes.
This study has six parts and a questionnaire. The individual parts of the study are independent of each other.

You will receive instructions on the screen. Please read the instructions carefully. If you have any questions, please raise your hand.

You will receive payment for your participation. During the study we will initially refer to points. At the end of the study all of the points will be exchanged for US Dollars.

The exchange rate: **1 point = $0.01**

You will receive part of the money immediately after this study and another part within four weeks.

You will receive a fixed sum of 600 points for taking part in the study (immediately afterwards). In addition, you will receive a variable amount of points for the different parts. This variable amount of points depends on your decisions and the decisions of other participants. The variable amount of points is paid out within four weeks. You will only receive a payment of points if you have thoroughly and completely processed the entire study. You will find out in the respective instructions to the different parts whether you can get points, and if yes, how.

The study will take approximately 60 minutes. You may only use the materials in front of you. Please only use the tablet as described in the instructions. You are not allowed to communicate with other participants. The use of cellphones is forbidden.

You can leave this study at any time. In that case you will not receive any payment.

If you have any questions now, please raise your hand.

Please click on "Next" to start the first part of the study.

Next

Figure A-1 Screenshot cheating experiment (1/8)

Part "DW"

Please take the pen and write out the following text on the paper with the heading "Part DW".
Subsequently, you will be asked a comprehension question on the text.

> Temperature is the measure of how hot or cold a thing is.
> Scientifically, temperature is a physical quantity which describes how quickly molecules are moving inside a material.
> In solids and liquids the molecules are vibrating around a fixed point in the substance, but in gases they are in free flight and bouncing off each other as they travel.

Once you have finished writing please click "Next".

Next

Figure A-2 Screenshot cheating experiment (2/8)

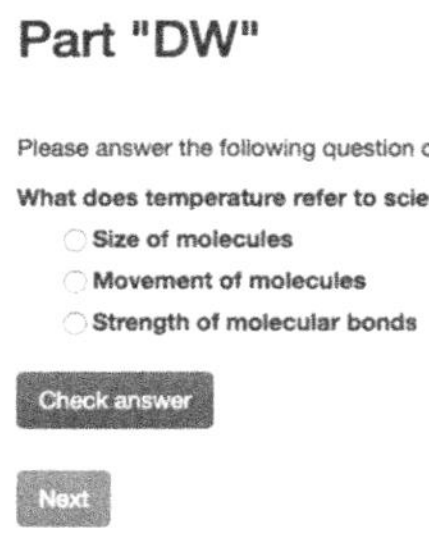

Figure A-3 Screenshot cheating experiment (3/8)

Figure A-4 Screenshot cheating experiment (4/8)

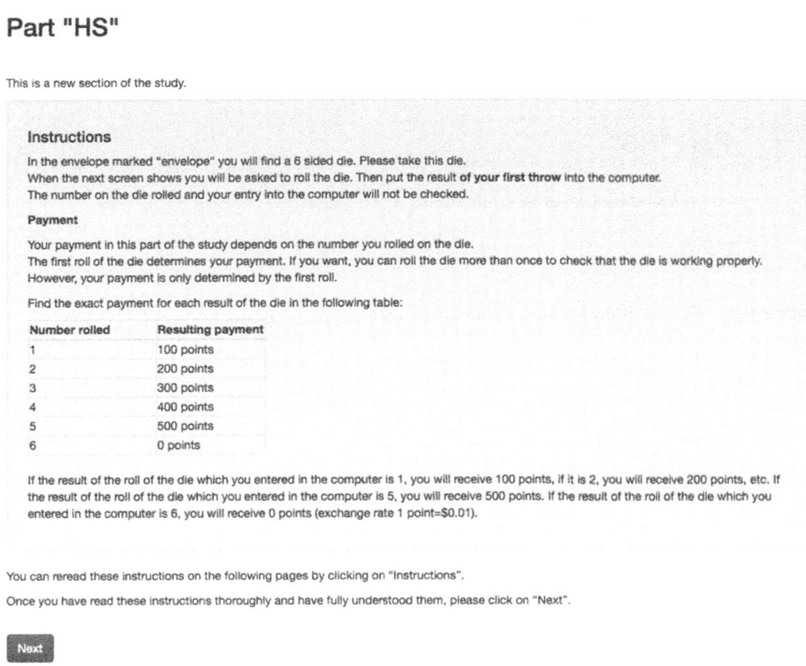

Figure A-5 Screenshot cheating experiment (5/8)

Figure A-6 Screenshot cheating experiment (6/8)

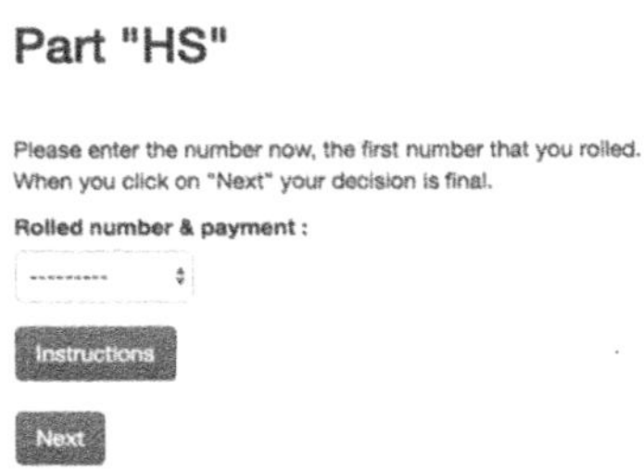

Figure A-7 Screenshot cheating experiment (7/8)

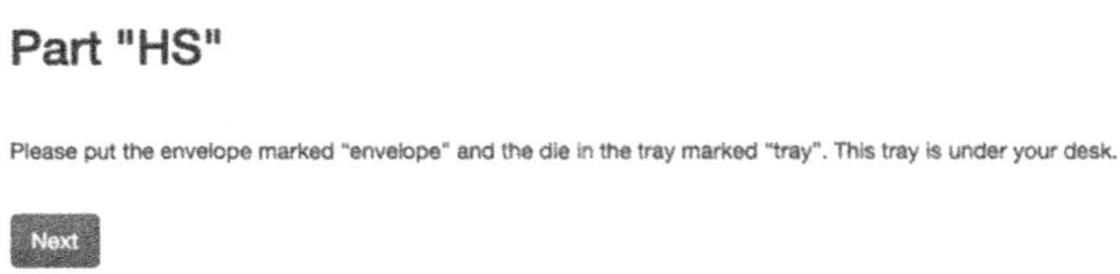

Figure A-8 Screenshot cheating experiment (8/8)

Appendix B: Supplement to "Foreign Language Effects on Creativity"

B.1 Overview of Participants

Table B-1 provides an overview of participant pools with mother tongues and processing languages. While a few participants were of different mother tongue than the common language at the respective university, all 430 participants from the dataset were randomly assigned to either mother tongue or treatment group.

Table B-1 Participant pools by location and language

Processing language *Mother tongue*	*German* *German*	*English* *German*	*French* *German*	*English* *English*	*German* *English*	*French* *French*	*German* *French*	**Total**
Ludwig Maximilians Universität	25	21	4		1	1		**52**
Universität Regensburg	23	20		2				**45**
Universität des Saarlandes	55	16	46			4	4	**125**
The Ohio State University		1		47	46			**94**
University of Wisconsin-Madison	1			15	17			**33**
Université Paris-Sorbonne	1		1			24	19	**45**
Université Sorbonne-Nouvelle	2		3			15	16	**36**
Total	**107**	**58**	**54**	**64**	**64**	**44**	**39**	**430**

B.2 Rating Procedures

The following paragraphs provide additional information on the web-based rating sessions, which were conducted to assess creativity.

S. Nothelfer, *Behavior in Foreign Languages*, Innovation und Entrepreneurship, https://doi.org/10.1007/978-3-658-31853-6

B.2.1 Randomization

Illustrations were rated in six bulks for operational reasons. Due to the between-subjects design and equal splits of each session into treatment and control, the treatment is randomized within each bulk. Yet, mother tongues correlate with the bulk structure. Each bulk was rated by a group of raters, randomly drawn from the same subject pools in France, Germany, and the United States. Within a bulk, raters were randomly assigned to illustrations. An algorithm ensured that no rater received the same illustration twice and that each illustration was assigned to two raters each from the German, French, and U.S. pool of raters (resulting in a total of six ratings per illustration). Furthermore, it ensured that the 20 illustrations used for rater training differed from the illustrations that were to rate. Depending on this random assignment, each rater rated between 47 and 50 illustrations. No potential rater was invited to participate in the rating more than once.

B.2.2 Procedures

All ratings were conducted online in web browsers. The rating task was programmed as oTree apps (Chen et al. 2014) and hosted on Heroku. Illustrations were hosted on Amazon S3. All communication and sessions were held in the language of the particular rater pool (in French for the French pool, German for the German pool, English for the U.S. pool). All materials were translated and back-translated from German (Brislin, 1970). Raters received an individual link and were given three days to complete the rating. They were asked to rate at a laptop, tablet, or desktop computer with a screen size of at least 10″ without interruptions. Furthermore, they were asked to rate alone and without any distractions (e.g., music, cell phone). Rater instructions included an explanation of the original illustration task with a picture of the available material. Before proceeding to the ratings, raters were shown 20 example illustrations as training to provide a reference for the ratings. Each illustration was rated on a 9-point discrete analog visual scale on creativity, quality of the technical execution, and aesthetics. Furthermore, raters were asked to name the object that was illustrated. Raters received a payment of 10 €/$ after completing the task.

B.2.3 Comparisons

Figure B-1 provides an overview of rating distributions by rater pool and participants' mother tongues. All three rater pools (US, Germany, France) show similar means and standard deviations in their creativity ratings (Germany: mean = 5.08 SD = 2.30; USA: mean = 4.99 SD = 2.44; France: mean = 5.05 SD = 2.24). Direct comparisons of the rater populations by their average creativity ratings for each image show no significant difference between the German and French rater pools (Wilcoxon signed-rank test $p = 0.32$) or between the French and US rater pools (Wilcoxon signed-rank test $p = 0.18$), but a significant difference between the German and US rater pools (Wilcoxon signed-rank test $p = 0.01$). As each illustration was rated by two randomly chosen raters of each rater group, the differences between German and US raters should not bias the results.

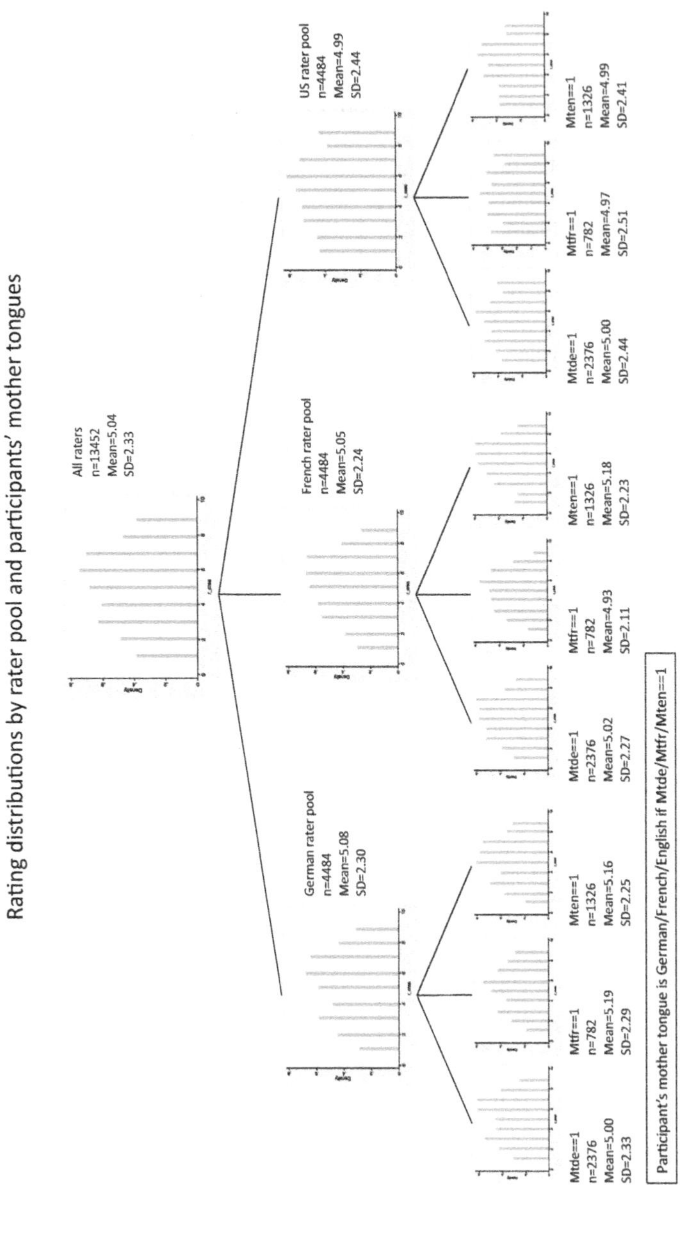

Figure B-1 Overview of rater pools

B.2.4 Rating Instructions

The following screenshots show the English version of the web-based rating session. Each image corresponds to one page displayed on the raters' browser. Please note that the logic behind buttons and input fields is not visible from these screenshots (Figures B-2, B-3, B-4, B-5, B-6 and B-7).

General information

Welcome to this study by the Max-Planck-Institute for Innovation and Competition in Munich in cooperation with Florida State University.

All details and decisions will be analyzed confidentially. The data will be used exclusively for academic purposes.

This study comprises a problem section and a questionnaire.

If you thoroughly and fully complete the study, you will receive remuneration. The payment upon completion of the study is $10.

The study will take approximately 30-45 minutes. The study must be completed without interruption. During the study, we also ask that you focus entirely on it and actively avoid any distractions (background music, cell phones etc.). Please complete the study on your own.

You can leave this study at any time. In that case you will not receive any payment.

Please click on "Next" to start the first part of the study.

Next

Figure B-2 Screenshot rating session (1/6)

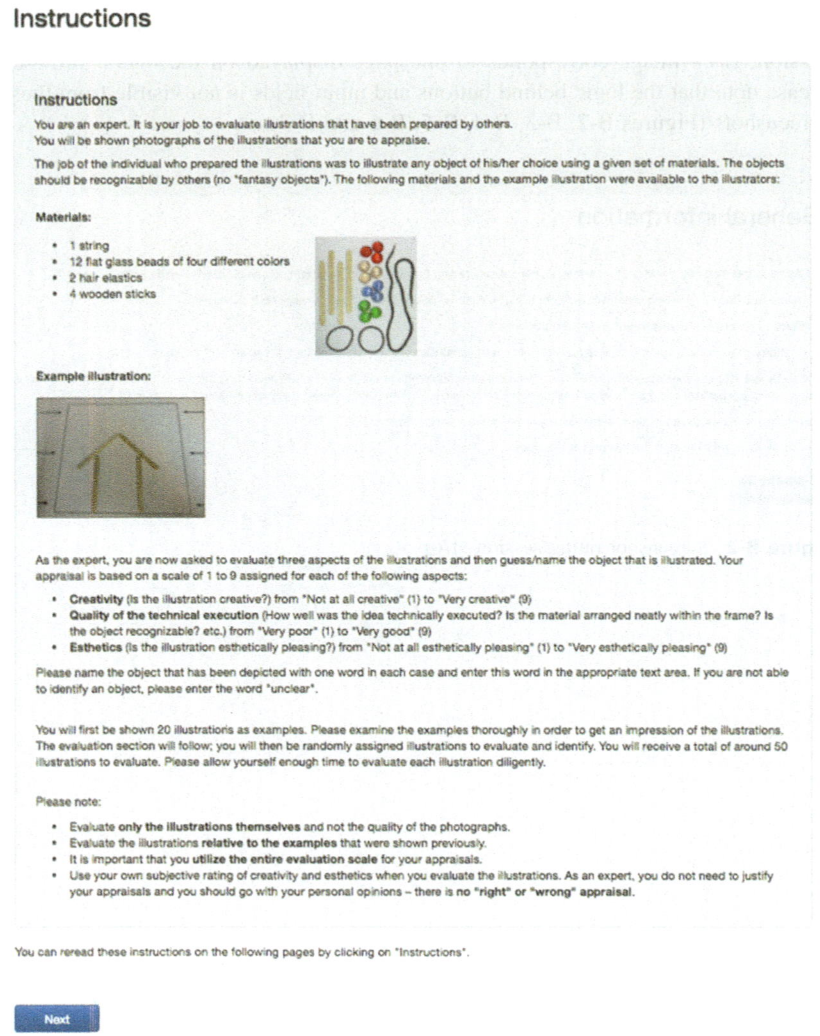

Instructions

Instructions

You are an expert. It is your job to evaluate illustrations that have been prepared by others.
You will be shown photographs of the illustrations that you are to appraise.

The job of the individual who prepared the illustrations was to illustrate any object of his/her choice using a given set of materials. The objects should be recognizable by others (no "fantasy objects"). The following materials and the example illustration were available to the illustrators:

Materials:

- 1 string
- 12 flat glass beads of four different colors
- 2 hair elastics
- 4 wooden sticks

Example illustration:

As the expert, you are now asked to evaluate three aspects of the illustrations and then guess/name the object that is illustrated. Your appraisal is based on a scale of 1 to 9 assigned for each of the following aspects:

- **Creativity** (Is the illustration creative?) from "Not at all creative" (1) to "Very creative" (9)
- **Quality of the technical execution** (How well was the idea technically executed? Is the material arranged neatly within the frame? Is the object recognizable? etc.) from "Very poor" (1) to "Very good" (9)
- **Esthetics** (Is the illustration esthetically pleasing?) from "Not at all esthetically pleasing" (1) to "Very esthetically pleasing" (9)

Please name the object that has been depicted with one word in each case and enter this word in the appropriate text area. If you are not able to identify an object, please enter the word "unclear".

You will first be shown 20 illustrations as examples. Please examine the examples thoroughly in order to get an impression of the illustrations. The evaluation section will follow; you will then be randomly assigned illustrations to evaluate and identify. You will receive a total of around 50 illustrations to evaluate. Please allow yourself enough time to evaluate each illustration diligently.

Please note:

- Evaluate **only the illustrations themselves** and not the quality of the photographs.
- Evaluate the illustrations **relative to the examples** that were shown previously.
- It is important that you **utilize the entire evaluation scale** for your appraisals.
- Use your own subjective rating of creativity and esthetics when you evaluate the illustrations. As an expert, you do not need to justify your appraisals and you should go with your personal opinions – there is **no "right" or "wrong" appraisal**.

You can reread these instructions on the following pages by clicking on "Instructions".

Next

Figure B-3 Screenshot rating session (2/6)

Figure B-4 Screenshot rating session (3/6)

Figure B-5 Screenshot rating session (4/6)

[19 additional examples were shown to the raters.]

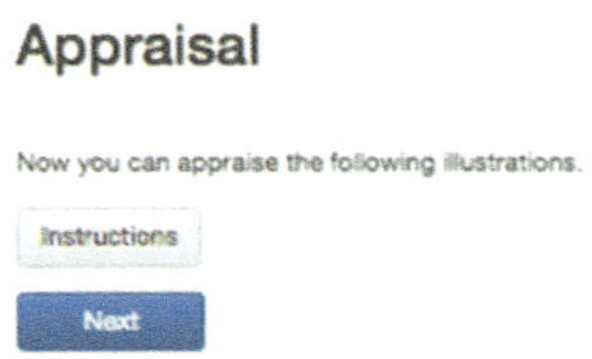

Figure B-6 Screenshot rating session (5/6)

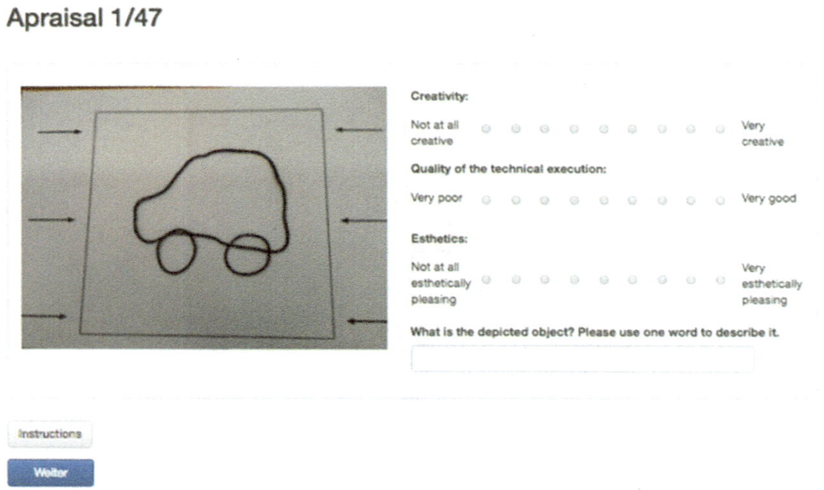

Figure B-7 Screenshot rating session (6/6)

[Raters have rated between 47 and 50 illustrations in total.]

B.3 Robustness Checks

B.3.1 Controlling for Rater Fixed Effects

The practice of rating in bulks yields correlations between individual raters and participants' mother tongues. Therefore, rater-specific differences, such as different anchor points, cannot be controlled for in regressions with the entire dataset without misestimating coefficients for mother tongue variables. As a robustness check, the OLS regressions in Table B-2 include rater fixed effects. While the coefficients for foreign language *fl* and for control variables should be estimated correctly, coefficients for *mtfr* and *mten* must not be interpreted due to collinearity with individual raters. Results are in line with regressions without rater fixed effects.

Table B-2 OLS regressions with rater fixed effects

OLS ALL	(8a) crea_all	(8b) crea_all	(9a) crea_top3	(9b) crea_top3	(10a) crea_top1	(10b) crea_top1
fl	-0.038 (0.092)	-0.046 (0.092)	0.026 (0.080)	0.018 (0.079)	0.015 (0.086)	0.008 (0.085)
mten		0.608*** (0.207)		0.623*** (0.188)		0.582* (0.316)
mtfr		-0.556** (0.243)		-0.656*** (0.208)		-0.567*** (0.218)
Rater Fixed Effects	Yes	Yes	Yes	Yes	Yes	Yes
Observations	13,842	13,842	7,548	7,548	2,580	2,580
R-squared	0.169	0.172	0.213	0.218	0.301	0.305

Robust standard errors clustered on creators in parentheses.
*** $p<0.01$, ** $p<0.05$, * $p<0.1$

Furthermore, the four individual sub-pools of participants with specific combinations of mother tongue and treatment language are analyzed separately. In these regressions, we cannot distinguish between a foreign language effect and language-specific effects, which might overlap or even cancel each other out. Accordingly, the *fl* coefficient should be interpreted as a general language effect in the OLS regressions in Table B-3, Table B-4, Table B-5, and Table B-6. Such a general language effect may include a foreign language effect, cultural language-specific effects, or both.

Table B-3 OLS regressions with participants of French mother tongue

OLS FRENCH MT	(9a) crea_all	(9b) crea_all	(10a) crea_top3	(10b) crea_top3	(11a) crea_top1	(11b) crea_top1
fl (German)	0.386**	0.301*	0.206	0.153	0.129	0.019
	(0.179)	(0.178)	(0.192)	(0.182)	(0.204)	(0.200)
Rater Fixed Effects	-	Yes	-	Yes	-	Yes
Constant	4.848***		5.560***		6.341***	
	(0.173)		(0.166)		(0.163)	
Observations	2,370	2,370	1,464	1,464	504	504
R-squared	0.007	0.235	0.002	0.243	0.001	0.362

Robust standard errors clustered on creators in parentheses.
*** p<0.01, ** p<0.05, * p<0.1

Table B-4 OLS regressions with German native speakers with French as foreign language

OLS GERMAN MT & FRENCH FL	(12a) crea_all	(12b) crea_all	(13a) crea_top3	(13b) crea_top3	(14a) crea_top1	(14b) crea_top1
fl (French)	-0.279	-0.292	-0.106	-0.130	-0.123	-0.297*
	(0.213)	(0.236)	(0.174)	(0.186)	(0.168)	(0.178)
Rater Fixed Effects	-	Yes	-	Yes	-	Yes
Constant	5.092***		5.946***		6.731***	
	(0.111)		(0.109)		(0.105)	
Observations	5,484	5,484	2,856	2,856	966	966
R-squared	0.003	0.171	0.001	0.233	0.001	0.374

Robust standard errors clustered on creators in parentheses.
*** p<0.01, ** p<0.05, * p<0.1

Table B-5 OLS regressions with German native speakers with English as foreign language

OLS GERMAN MT & ENGLISH FL	(15a) crea_all	(15b) crea_all	(16a) crea_top3	(16b) crea_top3	(17a) crea_top1	(17b) crea_top1
fl (English)	-0.154	-0.244	0.049	-0.062	0.083	-0.017
	(0.159)	(0.156)	(0.134)	(0.130)	(0.146)	(0.144)
Rater Fixed Effects	-	Yes	-	Yes	-	Yes
Constant	5.092***		5.946***		6.731***	
	(0.111)		(0.109)		(0.105)	
Observations	5,652	5,652	2,928	2,928	990	990
R-squared	0.001	0.168	0.000	0.239	0.000	0.370

Robust standard errors clustered on creators in parentheses.
*** p<0.01, ** p<0.05, * p<0.1

Table B-6 OLS regressions with participants of English mother tongue

OLS ENGLISH MT	(18a) crea_all	(18b) crea_all	(19a) crea_top3	(19b) crea_top3	(20a) crea_top1	(20b) crea_top1
fl (German)	0.056	0.093	0.054	0.089	0.151	0.226
	(0.133)	(0.125)	(0.148)	(0.135)	(0.166)	(0.159)
Rater Fixed Effects	-	Yes	-	Yes	-	Yes
Constant	5.095***		5.856***		6.573***	
	(0.139)		(0.148)		(0.163)	
Observations	3,978	3,978	2,232	2,232	768	768
R-squared	0.000	0.209	0.000	0.258	0.001	0.307

Robust standard errors clustered on creators in parentheses.
*** p<0.01, ** p<0.05, * p<0.1

B.3.2 Controlling for the Number of Illustrations

Table B-7 shows an OLS regression on creativity scores for all illustrations (models 21a_ctr–21c_ctr), the top-3 (22a_ctr–22c_ctr) and the top 1 (23a_ctr–23c_ctr) highest ranked illustrations, including a control for the amount of images (*total images*). Results show that previously observed effects for participants of French mother tongue are robust against controlling for the number of illustrations.

Table B-7 OLS regression including controls for the amount of images per participant

VARIABLES	(21a) crea_all	(21b) crea_all	(21c) crea_all	(22a) crea_top3	(22b) crea_top3	(22c) crea_top3	(23a) crea_top1	(23b) crea_top1	(23c) crea_top1
fl	0.002	-0.001	0.136	0.046	0.040	-0.036	0.070	0.061	-0.013
	(0.082)	(0.081)	(0.113)	(0.085)	(0.084)	(0.119)	(0.090)	(0.089)	(0.120)
mten		0.052	-0.015		-0.031	-0.079		-0.070	-0.149
		(0.145)	(0.169)		(0.147)	(0.177)		(0.151)	(0.188)
mtfr		-0.167	-0.433**		-0.240	-0.354*		-0.318*	-0.384**
		(0.162)	(0.190)		(0.157)	(0.190)		(0.168)	(0.188)
fl*mten			0.135			0.099			0.158
			(0.174)			(0.187)			(0.207)
fl*mtfr			0.564***			0.242			0.139
			(0.209)			(0.221)			(0.236)
total images	-0.157***	-0.161***	-0.160***	0.044*	0.037*	0.038*	0.007	-0.001	-0.001
	(0.021)	(0.021)	(0.020)	(0.022)	(0.022)	(0.022)	(0.023)	(0.023)	(0.023)
Constant	6.020***	6.060***	6.124***	5.604***	5.699***	5.732***	6.563***	6.698***	6.731***
	(0.147)	(0.156)	(0.157)	(0.148)	(0.158)	(0.163)	(0.162)	(0.168)	(0.166)
Observations	13,842	13,842	13,842	7,548	7,548	7,548	2,580	2,580	2,580
R-squared	0.028	0.029	0.030	0.002	0.004	0.004	0.000	0.004	0.005

Robust standard errors clustered on creators and raters in parentheses
*** p<0.01, ** p<0.05, * p<0.1

B.3.3 Controlling for Gender, Proficiency, Abroad Experience, and Order

Table B-8 adds several control variables to the models 1–3 (OLS regressions with all participants). Controls for *female, abroad experience,* and *order* are dummy variables. *Abroad experience* refers to having lived in a country, in which the foreign treatment language was used as the main language of communication. As the experiment comprises three different tasks that are varied in a 3 × 3 latin-square permutation, the two *order* dummies account for the creativity task in first and second place, leaving the third place to the baseline. *Proficiency* is based on self-ratings on a scale from 1 (very low) to 5 (very high). Results show that the patterns in models 1–3 are robust. Task order within the experiment appears to play a significant role, which is why we include regressions with a subgroup of participants who received the creativity task first (models 4–6).

Table B-8 OLS regressions with various controls and data from all participants

VARIABLES	(1a_ctr) crea_all	(1b_ctr) crea_all	(1c_ctr) crea_all	(2a_ctr) crea_top3	(2b_ctr) crea_top3	(2c_ctr) crea_top3	(3a_ctr) crea_top1	(3b_ctr) crea_top1	(3c_ctr) crea_top1
fl	-0.035	-0.033	-0.202	0.044	0.036	-0.031	0.062	0.053	-0.023
	(0.093)	(0.092)	(0.139)	(0.085)	(0.085)	(0.118)	(0.089)	(0.088)	(0.118)
mten		0.138	0.014		-0.059	-0.095		-0.089	-0.171
		(0.160)	(0.186)		(0.152)	(0.186)		(0.151)	(0.187)
mtfr		0.018	-0.247		-0.302*	-0.412**		-0.333**	-0.401**
		(0.170)	(0.201)		(0.157)	(0.187)		(0.169)	(0.187)
fl*mten			0.256			0.074			0.163
			(0.192)			(0.189)			(0.199)
fl*mtfr			0.565**			0.234			0.142
			(0.229)			(0.219)			(0.233)
female	0.092	0.117	0.127	0.160*	0.153*	0.156*	0.192*	0.178*	0.178*
	(0.104)	(0.108)	(0.106)	(0.092)	(0.091)	(0.090)	(0.106)	(0.104)	(0.103)
proficiency	-0.072	-0.059	-0.057	-0.078	-0.088*	-0.089*	-0.091	-0.105*	-0.107*
	(0.066)	(0.067)	(0.069)	(0.049)	(0.049)	(0.049)	(0.059)	(0.058)	(0.058)
abroad experience	0.132	0.136	0.121	0.103	0.134	0.133	0.034	0.066	0.063
	(0.107)	(0.106)	(0.105)	(0.099)	(0.098)	(0.098)	(0.099)	(0.098)	(0.098)
order crea first	-0.190	-0.181	-0.169	-0.129	-0.124	-0.118	-0.206*	-0.202*	-0.202*
	(0.116)	(0.115)	(0.114)	(0.108)	(0.107)	(0.107)	(0.113)	(0.112)	(0.112)
order crea second	-0.148	-0.139	-0.129	-0.099	-0.094	-0.090	-0.219*	-0.216*	-0.216*
	(0.114)	(0.113)	(0.112)	(0.108)	(0.108)	(0.108)	(0.117)	(0.117)	(0.117)
Constant	5.316***	5.190***	5.263***	6.073***	6.178***	6.211***	6.982***	7.122***	7.167***
	(0.310)	(0.337)	(0.354)	(0.242)	(0.256)	(0.266)	(0.301)	(0.305)	(0.305)
Observations	13,842	13,842	13,842	7,548	7,548	7,548	2,580	2,580	2,580
R-squared	0.003	0.004	0.006	0.003	0.006	0.007	0.007	0.011	0.011

OLS regression.Robust standard errors clustered on raters and creators in parentheses.
*** p<0.01, ** p<0.05, * p<0.1

B.3.4 Controlling for Gender, Proficiency, and Abroad Experience in a Reduced Subject Pool with Creativity as the First Task

Table B-9 adds several control variables to the models 4–6 (OLS regressions on a subset of participants that received the creativity task first). Control variables are identical to Table 4 of Chapter 3. Results show that the patterns in models 4–6 are robust. Being female and having abroad experience appear to positively affect creativity scores.

Table B-9 OLS regressions with controls and data from 155 participants who received the creativity task first

VARIABLES	(4a_ctr) crea_all	(4b_ctr) crea_all	(4c_ctr) crea_all	(5a_ctr) crea_top3	(5b_ctr) crea_top3	(5c_ctr) crea_top3	(6a_ctr) crea_top1	(6b_ctr) crea_top1	(6c_ctr) crea_top1
fl	0.272	0.252	0.223	0.246*	0.213	0.165	0.300*	0.265	0.108
	(0.171)	(0.171)	(0.262)	(0.147)	(0.148)	(0.210)	(0.164)	(0.166)	(0.231)
mten		0.197	0.362		-0.003	0.042		0.001	-0.132
		(0.238)	(0.299)		(0.203)	(0.277)		(0.229)	(0.320)
mtfr		-0.118	-0.343		-0.373*	-0.516**		-0.367	-0.555*
		(0.224)	(0.266)		(0.210)	(0.258)		(0.225)	(0.284)
fl*mten			-0.314			-0.076			0.255
			(0.366)			(0.337)			(0.370)
fl*mtfr			0.605			0.341			0.429
			(0.391)			(0.356)			(0.434)
female	0.346*	0.385*	0.379*	0.244	0.266	0.254	0.216	0.236	0.223
	(0.195)	(0.205)	(0.202)	(0.157)	(0.163)	(0.162)	(0.183)	(0.188)	(0.190)
proficiency	-0.027	-0.011	-0.014	-0.034	-0.042	-0.041	-0.092	-0.097	-0.103
	(0.118)	(0.115)	(0.115)	(0.079)	(0.077)	(0.077)	(0.099)	(0.099)	(0.101)
abroad experience	0.248	0.220	0.223	0.286*	0.263	0.257	0.079	0.056	0.042
	(0.169)	(0.171)	(0.175)	(0.162)	(0.163)	(0.164)	(0.167)	(0.168)	(0.170)
Constant	4.543***	4.448***	4.479***	5.484***	5.610***	5.642***	6.611***	6.728***	6.851***
	(0.557)	(0.587)	(0.620)	(0.367)	(0.391)	(0.417)	(0.459)	(0.498)	(0.541)
Observations	4,794	4,794	4,794	2,682	2,682	2,682	930	930	930
R-squared	0.010	0.011	0.015	0.009	0.014	0.015	0.011	0.016	0.018

OLS regression.Robust standard errors clustered on raters and creators in parentheses.

*** p<0.01, ** p<0.05, * p<0.1

B.4 Experimental Instructions

The following screenshots show an implementation of the creativity task in English, with a previous priming task. Each image corresponds to one page displayed on a tablet device in the mobile laboratory. Please note that the logic behind buttons and input fields is not visible from these screenshots (Figures B-8, B-9, B-10, B-11, B-12, B-13 and B-14).

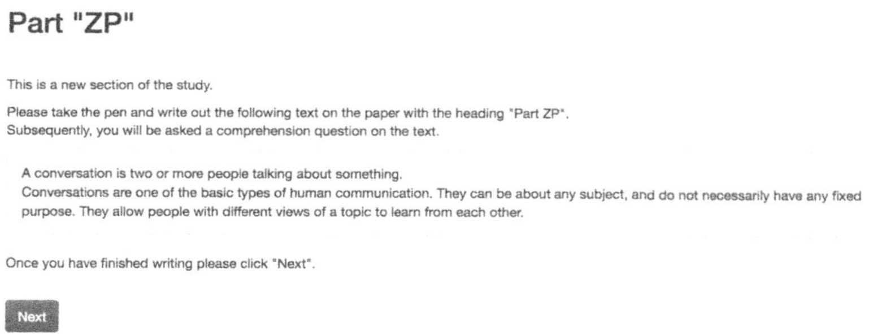

Figure B-8 Screenshot from the creativity experiment (1/7)

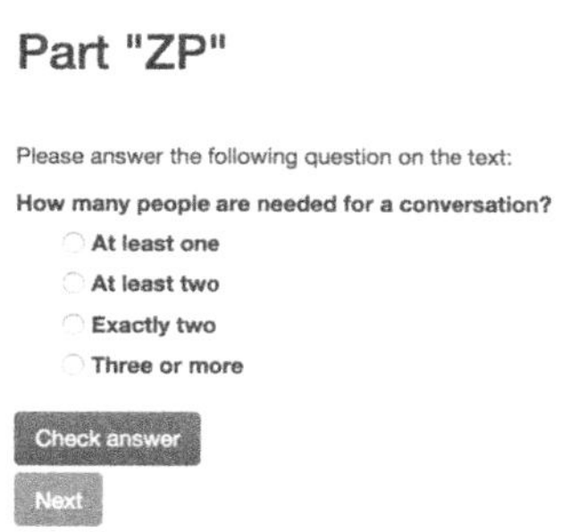

Figure B-9 Screenshot from the creativity experiment (2/7)

Figure B-10 Screenshot from the creativity experiment (3/7)

Part "TY"

This is a new section of the study.

In front of you is a work space and a closed box. Please **do not open the box, yet**. Open the box only when you are explicitly instructed to do so.

Task

Your task is to create illustrations of any objects of your choosing with the materials from the box. You illustrate objects of your choosing, photograph them, and submit them. Subsequently, your illustrations are rated. The rating determines your payment.

Details:

- You can illustrate whatever object you like; you can choose any object which comes to mind. There should only ever be **one** object in each illustration. The objects should be recognizable by others (no "fantasy objects").
- Use the work space marked in front of you to arrange the material into an illustration. You can use all of the materials or just some of the materials in the box. You are not allowed to use the box itself.
- Your illustration must not contain letters or numbers. Letters and numbers are forbidden.
- As soon as one illustration is finished, take a photo of it with the camera on the tablet and submit the photo. As soon as the photo has been submitted you can illustrate the next object of your choice.
- You have 10 minutes to illustrate various objects, take photos and submit them.

Example (illustrated object: House):

Evaluation

All of your illustrations will be evaluated by several other people after this study (referees). There is an international group of referees. Each referee evaluates the illustrations alone and is independent in their evaluation. Each referee evaluates:

- **Creativity** (Is your illustration creative?) on a 9-point scale from "Not creative at all" (1) to "Very creative"
- **Quality of the technical execution** (How well was your idea executed technically? Are the materials arranged neatly within the working area? Can the object be recognized? Etc.) on a 9-point scale from "Very poor" (1) to "Very good" (9)
- **Esthetics** (Is the illustration esthetically pleasing?) from "Not at all esthetically pleasing" (1) to "Very esthetically pleasing" (9)

Payment

Your payment is determined by the referees' **evaluation of your creativity**. For each illustration you get a value for creativity from the average mark given by the referees. **Your three most creative illustrations**, which rated highest on the creativity scale, determine the points you are paid. The following applies to each of your three most creative illustrations: for each point on the creativity scale you receive 20 points (exchange rate 1 point=€0.01).
The evaluations of both the quality of the technical execution and esthetics are not relevant to your payment.

You can reread these instructions on the following pages by clicking on "instructions".

Before you start the task, you need to test the camera and practice taking photos. Then comprehension questions follow. Do **not** open the box while practicing taking photos or answering comprehension questions. Open the box only when you are explicitly instructed to do so.

Once you have read the instructions and understood them fully, please click on "Next".

If you have any questions now, please raise your hand.

Next

Figure B-11 Screenshot from the creativity experiment (4/7)

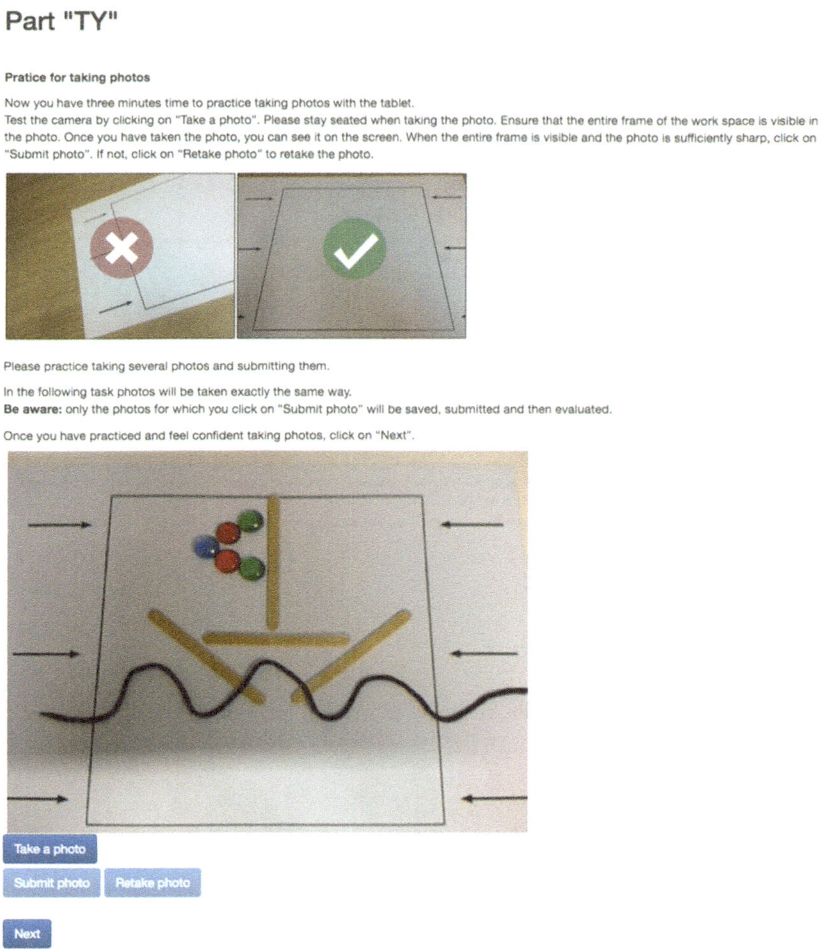

Figure B-12 Screenshot from the creativity experiment (5/7)

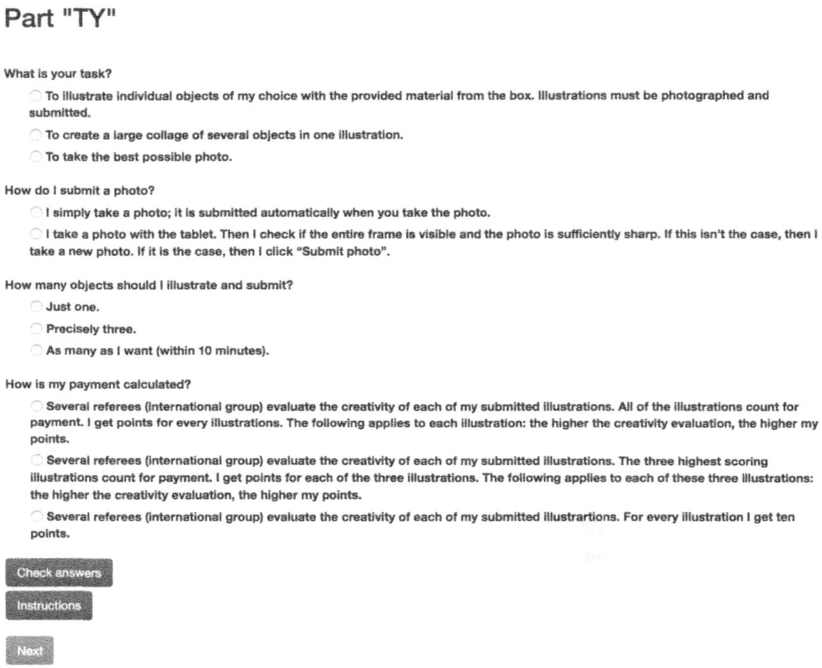

Part "TY"

What is your task?

- To illustrate individual objects of my choice with the provided material from the box. Illustrations must be photographed and submitted.
- To create a large collage of several objects in one illustration.
- To take the best possible photo.

How do I submit a photo?

- I simply take a photo; it is submitted automatically when you take the photo.
- I take a photo with the tablet. Then I check if the entire frame is visible and the photo is sufficiently sharp. If this isn't the case, then I take a new photo. If it is the case, then I click "Submit photo".

How many objects should I illustrate and submit?

- Just one.
- Precisely three.
- As many as I want (within 10 minutes).

How is my payment calculated?

- Several referees (international group) evaluate the creativity of each of my submitted illustrations. All of the illustrations count for payment. I get points for every illustrations. The following applies to each illustration: the higher the creativity evaluation, the higher my points.
- Several referees (international group) evaluate the creativity of each of my submitted illustrations. The three highest scoring illustrations count for payment. I get points for each of the three illustrations. The following applies to each of these three illustrations: the higher the creativity evaluation, the higher my points.
- Several referees (international group) evaluate the creativity of each of my submitted illustrartions. For every illustration I get ten points.

Check answers

Instructions

Next

Figure B-13 Screenshot from the creativity experiment (6/7)

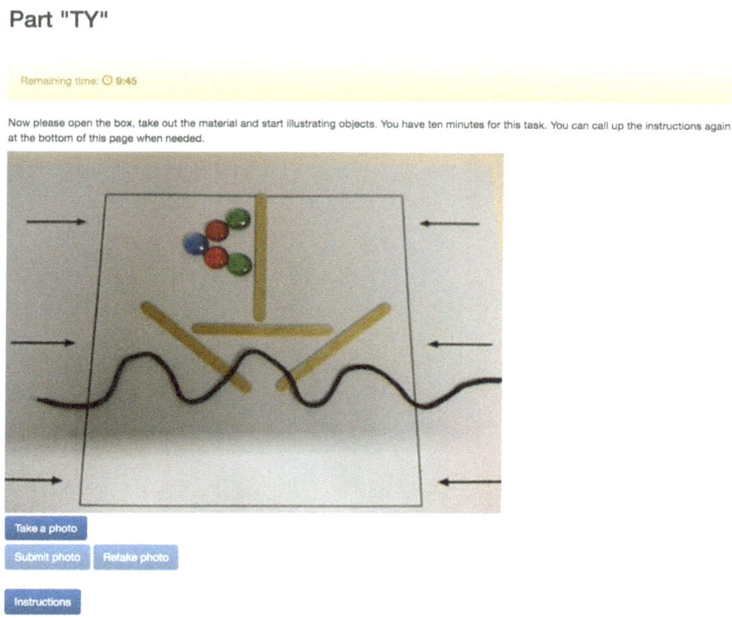

Figure B-14 Screenshot from the creativity experiment (7/7)

Appendix C: Supplement to "Cooperation in Foreign Languages"

C.1 Subgroup Analysis for a Potential Moderating Role of Abroad Experience

In order to analyze the role of abroad experience, we conducted regressions on subgroups. Results are presented in the following tables.

C.1.1 Participants with Abroad Experience

Table C-1 shows OLS regressions analogous to Table 3 of Chapter 4 for participants with abroad experience. On a first view, positive and significant coefficients for *fl* in models 7a, 7b, 7d, and 7e suggest an overall foreign language effect. However, when analyzing the language combinations in more detail (model 7c), this effect appears to be mainly driven by participants of German mother tongue who process in French (*fl* in model 7c), and partly by participants of French mother tongue who process in German (*fl* + *fl*mtfr* in model 7c, Wald test $p = 0.337$). The joint coefficient for participants of German mother tongue who process in English (*fl* + *en_mtde* in model 7c) is almost zero. For participants of English mother tongue who process in German, the joint coefficient (*fl* + *fl*mten*) is still positive and of decent effect size, but on a very low significance level (Wald test $p = 0.621$). When we introduce controls (model 7f), coefficients for *fl* and (*fl* + *fl*mtfr*) remain positive, while the previously positive coefficients in the English/German pairing vanish. In conclusion, we do not observe an overall foreign language effect contingent on abroad experience, but rather specific effects for French-German language pairings.

The potential moderating role of abroad experience is further investigated in a subgroup analysis of different mother tongues, which include participants with and without abroad experience. The coefficient of the interaction between abroad

S. Nothelfer, *Behavior in Foreign Languages*, Innovation und Entrepreneurship, https://doi.org/10.1007/978-3-658-31853-6

Table C-1 OLS regressions on transfers with data from participants with abroad experience only

OLS ABROAD EXP == 1	(7a) PD Transfer	(7b) PD Transfer	(7c) PD Transfer	(7d) PD Transfer	(7e) PD Transfer	(7f) PD Transfer
fl	22.719**	22.244*	49.720***	21.276*	19.853*	56.560***
	(11.356)	(11.391)	(17.204)	(11.034)	(11.138)	(16.981)
mten		6.248	14.563		11.130	27.952
		(13.919)	(20.557)		(13.650)	(19.846)
mtfr		-16.024	-13.215		-23.183	-22.079
		(13.592)	(17.730)		(14.099)	(17.457)
fl*mten			-38.035			-59.747**
			(28.948)			(27.738)
fl*mtfr			-27.642			-31.832
			(28.482)			(27.690)
en_mtde			-45.107**			-55.354***
			(20.500)			(19.601)
trust_std				-8.166	-5.059	-4.543
				(6.089)	(6.399)	(6.438)
altruism_std				21.316***	22.550***	23.731***
				(6.098)	(5.962)	(5.898)
risk_std				1.824	1.413	2.744
				(5.433)	(5.602)	(5.575)
age				1.627**	1.683***	1.959***
				(0.650)	(0.615)	(0.606)
female				-12.330	-10.311	-9.902
				(11.999)	(12.097)	(11.868)
proficiency				13.157**	13.872**	14.141**
				(6.066)	(5.968)	(6.072)
order: pd third				-18.447	-17.791	-15.629
				(13.375)	(13.431)	(13.146)
order: pd first				3.567	6.963	10.066
				(14.971)	(14.717)	(14.812)
Constant	179.781***	181.999***	179.137***	100.396***	96.272***	82.031**
	(8.120)	(9.959)	(11.466)	(35.241)	(34.600)	(35.494)
Observations	273	273	273	273	273	273
R-squared	0.015	0.022	0.037	0.110	0.125	0.151

OLS Regression. Participants with abroad experience only. Robust standard errors in parentheses.
*** $p<0.01$, ** $p<0.05$, * $p<0.1$

experience and foreign language processing *fl*abroad experience* estimates the moderating effect.

C.1.2 Participants of French Mother Tongue

Table C-2 shows OLS regressions on transfers and expected transfers with data from participants of French mother tongue only. Results show a strong moderating effect of abroad experience for both transfer and expectations. Overall, processing in German has almost no effect on transfers (*fl* in model 8a) and a positive yet insignificant coefficient for expected transfers (*fl* in model 9a). For participants without abroad experience in a German-speaking country, processing in German has a significant negative effect on transfers (*fl* in models 8b-c), and an insignificant yet negative coefficient on expected transfers (*fl* in models 9b-c). For participants with abroad experience, processing in German has no significant effect on transfers (*fl + fl*abroad experience* in model 8b, Wald test $p = 0.358$) and a significantly positive effect of considerable size on expected transfers (*fl + fl*abroad experience* in model 9b, Wald test $p = 0.040$).

The moderating effect itself is statistically significant and of highly positive effect size for both transfers and expectations (*fl*abroad experience* in models 8b-c and 9b-c).

Table C-2 OLS regressions on transfer and expected transfer with data from French native speakers only

OLS FRENCH MT	(8a) Transfer	(8b) Transfer	(8c) Transfer	(9a) Exp. Transf.	(9b) Exp. Transf.	(9c) Exp. Transf.
fl	-3.692	-88.333**	-85.933**	24.205	-50.833	-49.487
	(21.160)	(39.691)	(39.635)	(19.849)	(35.733)	(41.708)
abroad experience		1.364	1.557		-27.500	-20.551
		(25.511)	(27.098)		(26.022)	(29.142)
fl*abroad exprience		109.970**	104.339**		98.833**	88.842*
		(45.973)	(46.959)		(42.459)	(46.044)
trust_std			1.579			3.210
			(10.694)			(10.260)
altruism_std			28.249***			15.810
			(10.658)			(10.130)
risk_std			2.376			13.555
			(10.018)			(11.274)
age			0.703			-0.613
			(1.074)			(1.150)
female			-18.146			-4.892
			(22.805)			(22.070)
proficiency			-7.718			-16.130
			(11.174)			(11.411)
order: pd third			4.857			-15.275
			(23.494)			(24.157)
order: pd first			-9.316			-8.821
			(29.172)			(27.743)
Constant	166.000***	165.000***	184.852***	157.333***	177.500***	259.623***
	(11.632)	(21.279)	(64.618)	(12.114)	(21.573)	(72.478)
Observations	84	84	84	84	84	84
R-squared	0.000	0.118	0.247	0.018	0.081	0.180

Robust standard errors in parentheses
*** p<0.01, ** p<0.05, * p<0.1

C.1.3 Participants of German Mother Tongue and French as Foreign Language

Table C-3 shows OLS regressions on transfers and expected transfers with data from participants of German mother tongue who process in either German or French. Overall, processing in French has a significantly positive effect on transfers of German native speakers (*fl* in model 10a) and shows a positive, yet insignificant coefficient for expected transfers (*fl* in model 11a). For participants without abroad experience, processing in French has insignificant positive coefficients for transfers (*fl* in models 10b-c) and expected transfers (*fl* in models 11b-c). For participants with abroad experience, processing in French has a strongly significant positive effect on transfers (*fl* + *fl*abroad experience* in model 10b, Wald test p = 0.004) and no significant effect on expected transfers (*fl* + *fl*abroad experience* in model 11b, Wald test p = 0.670).

The moderating effect itself is positive, yet insignificant for transfers, and negative, yet insignificant for expectations (*fl*abroad experience* in models 10b-c and 11b-c).

Table C-3 OLS regressions on transfer and expected transfer with data from German native speakers who processed in German or French only

OLS GERMAN MT & FRENCH FL	(10a) Transfer	(10b) Transfer	(10c) Transfer	(11a) Exp. Transf.	(11b) Exp. Transf.	(11c) Exp. Transf.
fl	36.646**	11.842	21.611	19.107	37.895	44.288*
	(14.273)	(24.954)	(25.454)	(16.242)	(25.984)	(26.482)
abroad experience		-9.989	-18.327		7.551	1.844
		(18.380)	(18.847)		(18.522)	(17.825)
fl*abroad exprience		38.319	35.424		-29.025	-27.239
		(30.360)	(30.252)		(33.276)	(33.077)
trust_std			-1.791			-5.895
			(8.669)			(9.526)
altruism_std			13.610*			14.005*
			(7.832)			(8.143)
risk_std			14.225*			17.677**
			(7.327)			(7.870)
age			0.373			1.209
			(1.100)			(1.267)
female			-41.352***			-14.751
			(14.665)			(16.791)
proficiency			12.518			10.330
			(8.013)			(8.270)
order: pd third			-22.016			-9.518
			(18.262)			(20.063)
order: pd first			-27.995			-17.443
			(20.447)			(22.119)
Constant	182.243***	188.684***	179.191***	156.449***	151.579***	103.338**
	(8.990)	(14.252)	(47.043)	(9.002)	(14.477)	(51.539)
Observations	161	161	161	161	161	161
R-squared	0.037	0.046	0.150	0.009	0.014	0.081

Robust standard errors in parentheses
*** p<0.01, ** p<0.05, * p<0.1

C.1.4 Participants of German Mother Tongue and English as Foreign Language

Table C-4 shows OLS regressions on transfers and expected transfers with data from participants of German mother tongue that process in either German or English. Overall, processing in English does not affect transfers (*fl* in model 12a) or expected transfers (*fl* in model 13a).

Table C-4 OLS regressions on transfer and expected transfer with data from German native speakers who processed in German or English only

OLS GERMAN MT & ENGLISH FL	(12a) Transfer	(12b) Transfer	(12c) Transfer	(13a) Exp. Transf.	(13b) Exp. Transf.	(13c) Exp. Transf.
fl	5.516	4.008	10.390	0.793	13.421	21.722
	(15.590)	(25.138)	(26.038)	(15.027)	(25.592)	(25.274)
abroad experience		-9.989	-13.861		7.551	2.089
		(18.375)	(19.070)		(18.516)	(17.944)
fl*abroad exprience		1.046	-9.892		-21.614	-33.880
		(31.967)	(34.209)		(31.192)	(31.419)
trust_std			11.053			9.627
			(9.393)			(8.390)
altruism_std			4.684			2.244
			(9.501)			(8.732)
risk_std			12.376			17.443**
			(7.717)			(7.299)
age			0.955			1.135
			(1.305)			(1.319)
female			-12.047			4.507
			(16.689)			(15.668)
proficiency			8.513			12.246
			(8.128)			(8.698)
order: pd third			-33.655*			-29.341
			(19.832)			(18.989)
order: pd first			-1.447			1.251
			(20.467)			(19.895)
Constant	182.243***	188.684***	155.694***	156.449***	151.579***	85.114
	(8.989)	(14.248)	(50.049)	(9.001)	(14.472)	(51.870)
Observations	165	165	165	165	165	165
R-squared						

OLS Regression. Robust standard errors in parentheses
*** p<0.01, ** p<0.05, * p<0.1

The coefficients of *fl*abroad experience* indicate no strong moderating role of abroad experience on transfers (models 12b-c), and a potential negative, yet insignificant moderating role on expected transfers (models 13b-c).

C.1.5 Participants of English Mother Tongue

Table C-5 shows OLS regressions on transfers and expected transfers with data from participants of English mother tongue who process in German only. Overall, processing in German seems to not affect transfers (*fl* in model 14a) and has a positive, yet insignificant coefficient for expected transfers (*fl* in model 15a).

For participants without abroad experience, processing in German appears to have no effect on transfers (*fl* in models 14b-c), and a potentially negative, yet insignificant, effect on expected transfers (*fl* in models 15b-c). For participants with abroad experience, processing in German has a slightly more positive, yet insignificant, coefficient for transfers (*fl* + *fl*abroad experience* in model 14b, Wald test p = 0.611) and a strongly positive significant effect on expected transfers (*fl* + *fl*abroad experience* in model 15b, Wald test p = 0.037).

The moderating effect itself is positive, yet insignificant for transfers, and positive and significant for expectations (*fl*abroad experience* in models 14b-c and 15b-c).

Table C-5 OLS regressions on transfer and expected transfer with data from English native speakers only

OLS ENGLISH MT	(14a) Transfer	(14b) Transfer	(14c) Transfer	(15a) Exp. Transf.	(15b) Exp. Transf.	(15c) Exp. Transf.
fl	3.281	-10.329	-0.111	22.500	-30.857	-19.204
	(18.136)	(28.687)	(30.450)	(21.070)	(30.548)	(32.050)
abroad experience		-0.595	-5.929		-37.857	-46.149
		(26.762)	(28.372)		(31.538)	(32.511)
fl*abroad exprience		22.380	-2.895		90.473**	65.015
		(37.185)	(39.184)		(41.599)	(42.345)
trust_std			-0.302			26.416**
			(11.081)			(10.974)
altruism_std			17.406*			19.945*
			(10.090)			(10.996)
risk_std			4.149			16.816
			(10.040)			(10.708)
age			3.869***			2.494
			(1.411)			(2.284)
female			-4.631			11.492
			(19.231)			(20.882)
proficiency			23.209**			28.929***
			(10.823)			(10.889)
order: pd third			11.937			-7.754
			(21.894)			(24.704)
order: pd first			34.215			24.403
			(23.260)			(26.099)
Constant	193.594***	193.929***	14.854	141.562***	162.857***	-2.728
	(13.143)	(20.218)	(56.918)	(15.761)	(23.318)	(68.404)
Observations	128	128	128	128	128	128
R-squared	0.000	0.006	0.135	0.009	0.045	0.227

Robust standard errors in parentheses
*** p<0.01, ** p<0.05, * p<0.1

C.2 Survey Items for Trust, Altruism, and Risk Propensity

General attitudes towards trusting others are elicited with three statements (see Table C-6). Numerical coding of the answers reflects an increase in trust with increasing numbers. Altruism is elicited with a self-assessment on a visual analog scale (*altruism 1*), a virtual situation (*altruism 2*), and the level of agreement to a statement (*altruism 3*). The willingness to take risks is assessed with a self-assessment on a visual analog scale. Numerical coding reflects increasing altruism with increasing numbers. Aggregate variables of trust (*trust_std*) and altruism (*altruism_std*) are standardized sums of single variables, taking into account differences answer scales.

Table C-6 Elicitation of trust, altruism, and willingness to take risks

	Variable	*Question / Description*	*Answer Range / Formula*
Trust			
	trust1	[What is your opinion on the following statements?] You can trust people in general.	Strongly agree (4) Somewhat agree (3) Somewhat disagree (2) Strongly disagree (1)
	trust2	[What is your opinion on the following statements?] You cannot rely on anyone these days.	Strongly agree (1) Somewhat agree (2) Somewhat disagree (3) Strongly disagree (4)
	trust3	[What is your opinion on the following statements?] When you are dealing with strangers, it is better to be careful before you trust them.	Strongly agree (1) Somewhat agree (2) Somewhat disagree (3) Strongly disagree (4)
	trust_std	Standardized (mean=0; SD=1) sum of trust1-3	trust_std=std(trust1+trust2+trust3)
Altruism			
	altruism1	How do you estimate your willingness to share without expecting anything in return (e.g. willingness to donate)?	Not willing at all (1) ... Very willing (7)
	altruism2	Imagine this hypothetical situation. If you won 300 Dollars how much of it would you donate?	none (1) 25% (2) 50% (3) 75% (4) all (5)
	altruism3	I cannot understand how people waste their time fighting for an aim which doesn't give them any direct benefit.	Strongly agree (4) Somewhat agree (3) Somewhat disagree (2) Strongly disagree (1)
	altruism_std	Standardized (mean=0; SD=1) sum of altruism1-3, accounting for different scale levels	altruism_std=std((altruism1-1)/6+(altruism2-1)/4+(altruismt3-1)/3)
Risk			
	risk	What's your personal assessment: are you generally someone who is willing to take risks or you do avoid risks?	Not willing to take risks at all (1) ... Very willing to take risks (10)
	risk_std	Standardized risk propensity	risk_std=std(risk)

C.3 Experimental Instructions

The following screenshots show instructions in the English version of the experiment. Each image corresponds to one page displayed on a tablet device in the mobile lab. The logic behind buttons and input fields is not visible from these screenshots. For example, clicking on a button labeled "Instructions" opens a modal window with the previously given instructions. Participants start with a priming task, followed by the prisoner's dilemma (Figures C-1, C-2, C-3, C-4, C-5, C-6, C-7 and C-8).

General Information

Welcome to this study by the Max-Planck-Institute for Innovation and Competition in Munich in cooperation with The Ohio State University.
This study has no bearing on your program of study and does not affect your grades.
All details and decisions will be analyzed confidentially. The data will be used exclusively for academic purposes.
This study has six parts and a questionnaire. The individual parts of the study are independent of each other.

You will receive instructions on the screen. Please read the instructions carefully. If you have any questions, please raise your hand.

You will receive payment for your participation. During the study we will initially refer to points. At the end of the study all of the points will be exchanged for US Dollars.

The exchange rate: **1 point = $0.01**

You will receive part of the money immediately after this study and another part within four weeks.

You will receive a fixed sum of 600 points for taking part in the study (immediately afterwards). In addition, you will receive a variable amount of points for the different parts. This variable amount of points depends on your decisions and the decisions of other participants. The variable amount of points is paid out within four weeks. You will only receive a payment of points if you have thoroughly and completely processed the entire study. You will find out in the respective instructions to the different parts whether you can get points, and if yes, how.

The study will take approximately 60 minutes. You may only use the materials in front of you. Please only use the tablet as described in the instructions. You are not allowed to communicate with other participants. The use of cellphones is forbidden.

You can leave this study at any time. In that case you will not receive any payment.

If you have any questions now, please raise your hand.

Please click on "Next" to start the first part of the study.

Next

Figure C-1 Screenshot from cooperation experiment (1/8)

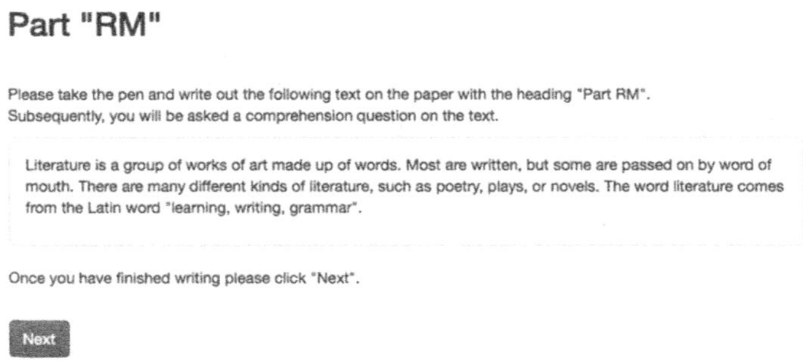

Figure C-2 Screenshot from cooperation experiment (2/8)

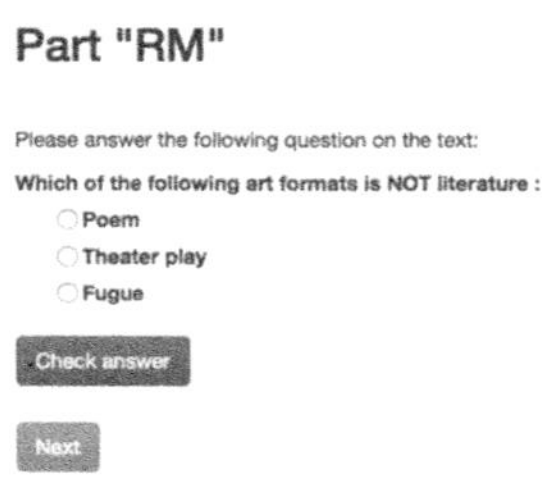

Figure C-3 Screenshot from cooperation experiment (3/8)

Figure C-4 Screenshot from cooperation experiment (4/8)

Part "KF"

This is a new section of the study.

Instructions

In this part of the study, you will be assigned to another participant. The other participant is of this session, or of another session with participants from your university. This assignment will be at random. The participant assigned to you (hereafter the "other participant") will have exactly the same instructions as you.

The other participant makes an identically structured decision as you.

For each decision each participant will get a starting amount of 300 points (exchange rate 1 point=$0.01). From the starting amount you can transfer any amount of points to the other participant (in 30 point steps). Thus, you can choose the following amounts [0, 30, 60, 90, 120, 150, 180, 210, 240, 270, or 300 points].

The amount that you transfer to the other participant is doubled. That means that the other participant receives twice as much as what you transferred to the other participant.

The other participant has exactly the same choice as you do. The other participant can transfer any amount to you. The amount that the other participant transfers to you is also doubled. That means that you will receive twice as much as what the other participant has transferred to you.

You and the other participant make your decisions independent of each other. That means that you do not know how many points the other participant transfers to you when you make your decision. The other participant also does not know how many points you transfer to them before he or she makes their decision. You and the other participant make this decision just once. There is no repeated interaction with the other participant.

Payment

Your payment amount depends on your decision and the decision made by the other participant.

Starting amount
minus the amount you transferred to the other participant
plus the doubled amount that the other participant transferred to you
= **Your personal payment**

You can reread these instructions on the following pages by clicking on "instructions".

There are a few comprehension questions.

Next

Figure C-5 Screenshot from cooperation experiment (5/8)

Figure C-6 Screenshot from cooperation experiment (6/8)

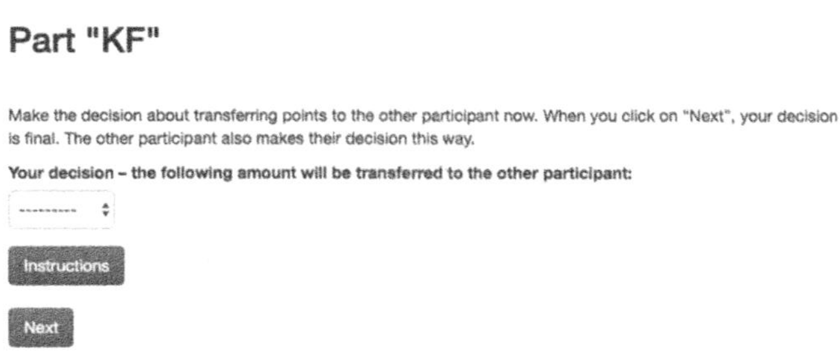

Figure C-7 Screenshot from cooperation experiment (7/8)

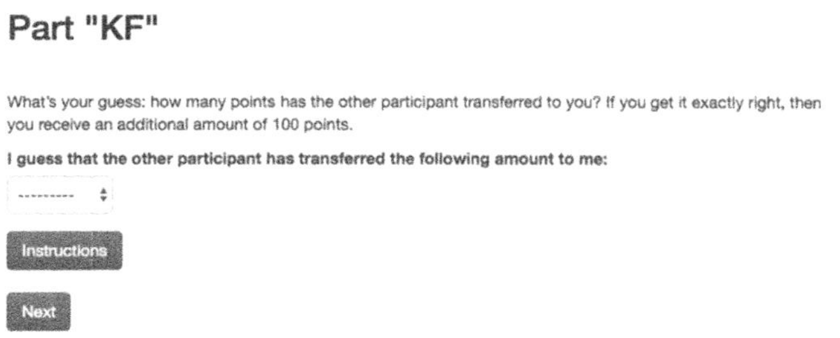

Figure C-8 Screenshot from cooperation experiment (8/8)

Appendix D: Supplement to "The Mobile Laboratory"

D.1 General Setup

In order to ensure comparable environmental conditions across the different locations and to be able to conduct experiments without having to rely on local laboratories, I specifically designed and built a mobile laboratory for the experimental series[1]. The following paragraphs outline the general setup of the laboratory system including some technical details that may prove useful for similar applications in the future.

The mobile laboratory consists of modified tablet devices for instructions and inputs, wireless network infrastructure, a server to run the experimental software and to store data, a laptop for session control, numbered testing dividers for each seat, experiment-specific materials, and rugged cases for easy and safe transportation. In the used configuration, it can accommodate up to 24 participants per session. The system is versatile and can be used at any location with sufficiently large tables and electricity. It has been designed to be easily transportable by car or airplane. Figure D-1 illustrates how the mobile laboratory looks in practice.

D.2 Technical Infrastructure

The following paragraphs provide more details on the technical aspects of the mobile laboratory and procedures.

---

[1] I would like to thank Nathalie Eisenhut for her valuable contribution of adding multimedia support to the system, as well as Marco Kleine and all volunteers involved in beta-testing the system at the Center for Digital Technology and Management, Munich, for providing invaluable feedback and constructive ideas.

S. Nothelfer, *Behavior in Foreign Languages*, Innovation und Entrepreneurship,
https://doi.org/10.1007/978-3-658-31853-6

Figure D-1 The mobile laboratory on site

D.2.1 Tablet Devices

Each participant has a tablet device (Microsoft Surface 3 or Microsoft Surface 4 Pro) to click through the tasks and enter data. The tablets run on Windows and have been modified to match experimental requirements. System settings are configured in the desired treatment language, and all input- and language-related features that could interfere with the experiment are deactivated (e.g., auto-update, auto-correct, auto-fill). Furthermore, energy saving features such as the activation of standby mode after a certain time and screensavers are deactivated. The windows registry is modified to auto-sign into the experimental user profile without having to enter a password.

In order to run the experimental tasks in a browser, each device has a pre-configured installation of version 52 or older[2] of Google Chrome in the desired treatment language. Any Google Chrome features that could interfere with the experiments are deactivated (e.g., translation services, auto-fill, auto-correct).

All tablets are connected to a wireless network with static IP addresses, which facilitates troubleshooting (Figure D-2).

[2]More recent versions of Chrome do not support all command line flags that are required for camera access and kiosk mode.

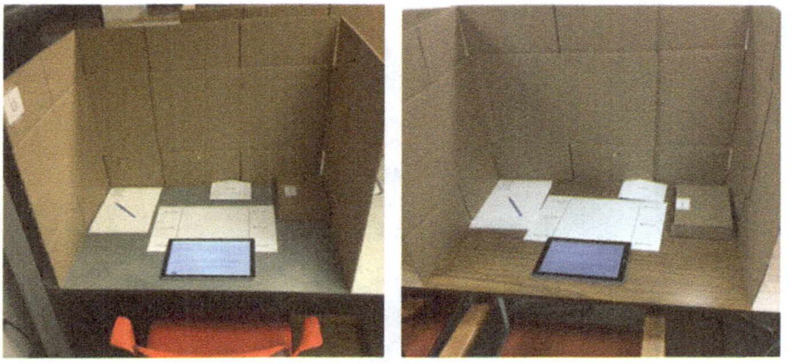

Figure D-2 Participant seats with tablet devices at different locations

D.2.2 Network

The experiment runs in an own WPA2-secured private network without connection to the internet. The network is span with a high-performance wireless router in two channels, in order to minimize latency and issues with signal strength or interference. Apart from the tablet devices and a server, at least one additional device is connected to the network for session control.

D.2.3 Server

The server is a regular laptop computer that operates on Ubuntu. It runs a Daphne server with the platform oTree (Chen, Schonger, & Wickens, 2016) and all experimental apps. Also, a standard Apache fileserver is used to serve and store media content such as photos.

Data is stored only on a server laptop that runs the experimental system. At no point in time is any data stored locally on the tablets. Accordingly, the data is secure even in cases of missing tablet devices (Figure D-3).

Figure D-3 Technical components of the mobile laboratory

D.3 Experimental Software

The laboratory relies on the open-source experimental platform oTree (Chen, Schonger, & Wickens, 2016). oTree is browser-based and hence allows to run experimental apps on any device with a web browser. Perhaps most importantly, it has the advantage of relying on standard web-development frameworks (Python, Django, Bootstrap), which makes it customizable.

Each experimental task has been programmed as an oTree app. In order to account for the different languages, each task has been programmed in a separate app for each language. Due to the nature of this study, I had to circumvent oTree's default language setting, which has been achieved with customizations of predefined elements such as buttons or currency symbols.

For some tasks such as the creativity task, the default oTree framework has been extended with custom-built modules for accessing the tablet cameras, as well as to enable real-time multimedia support for sending and receiving media to and from the Apache server. These customizations were made with standard tools for web-design (JavaScript/JQuery, Ajax, etc.).

D.4 Session Procedures

After assembly of the laboratory in a suitable room and preparation of the seats with the task-specific material, sessions are initiated in the web browser of a standard laptop using oTree's session control functions. Due to the between-subjects design with two languages in each session, two separate oTree sessions were initiated simultaneously for one experimental session. When initiating a session, oTree generates session-specific hyperlinks to access the experiments via web-browsers.

The mobile laboratory relies on batch files to access the correct experimental task in kiosk mode from each tablet device. Session-specific hyperlinks are copied into Batch-files that are shared on the session control laptop via standard file-sharing. These batch-files are then executed on each client device to start the experiment.

When executed, the batch-files start Google Chrome with the desired hyperlink to the app with additional command line flags. The command line flags enable kiosk mode (i.e., the browser is launched in full-screen and address lines, buttons, etc. are not visible), and circumvent security features to enable access to the back camera of the tablet for taking pictures. Furthermore, the batch-file contains a command to kill the tablet's explorer.exe process, to deactivate any physical buttons or possible gesture input that could let users exit the experimental app. Figure D-4 shows the code of an exemplary batch-file with corresponding command line flags.

```
taskkill /f /im explorer.exe

start C:\"Program Files (x86)"\Google\Chrome\Application\chrome.exe ^

--unsafely-treat-insecure-origin-as-secure="http://192.168.1.101:8000" ^

--user-data-dir="C:\Users\otree\AppData\Local\Google\Chrome\User Data\Default" ^

--kiosk http://192.168.1.101:8000/join/0kycdxc9bh/ ^

--use-fake-ui-for-media-stream ^
```

Figure D-4 Exemplary batch file for launching the experiment in kiosk mode

The experimental app is launched in full-screen mode on the tablets and participants are locked-in. The single interface for interactions and data input is the touchscreen. In order to leave the experimental app after a session is finished, a physical type-cover is required. Once the external keyboard is connected, one can either restart the explorer.exe process, or reboot the device.

During the session, the oTree session control is used to monitor the participant's progress and identify potential problems. After the session, data is retrieved from the server laptop and securely stored in an encrypted cloud storage. In the described experimental series, each laboratory session yields six datasets in csv format and a variable number of images in jpg format. For analysis, all datasets are merged into one, using session codes and variable names as identifiers.

References

Adamson, R. E. (1952). Functional fixedness as related to problem solving: A repetition of three experiments. *Journal of experimental psychology, 44*(4), 288–291.

Akkermans, D., Harzing, A. W., & van Witteloostuijn, A. (2010). Cultural accommodation and language priming. *Management international review, 50*(5), 559–583.

Amabile, T. M. (1988). A model of creativity and innovation in organizations. *Research in organizational behavior, 10*(1), 123–167.

Amabile, T. M. (1996). Creativity in context: Update to the social psychology of creativity. Boulder, CO: Westview press.

Andreoni, J. (1990). Impure altruism and donations to public goods: A theory of warm-glow giving. *The economic journal, 100*(401), 464–477.

Ashby, F. G., Valentin, V. V., & Turken, A. U. (2002). The effects of positive affect and arousal on working memory and executive attention. In: Moore, S., & Oaksford, M. (Eds.). *Emotional Cognition: From Brain to Behaviour* (pp. 245–287). Amsterdam: John Benjamins Publishing Company.

Athanasopoulos, P., & Aveledo, F. (2013). Linguistic relativity and bilingualism. In: Altarriba, J., & Isurin, L. (Eds.). (pp. 236–255). *Memory, language, and bilingualism: theoretical and applied approaches*. Cambridge: Cambridge University Press.

Baas, M., De Dreu, C. K., & Nijstad, B. A. (2008). A meta-analysis of 25 years of mood-creativity research: Hedonic tone, activation, or regulatory focus? *Psychological bulletin, 134*(6), 779.

Balliet, D., Wu, J., & De Dreu, C. K. (2014). In-group favoritism in cooperation: a meta-analysis. *Psychological bulletin, 140*(6), 1556.

Bartolotti, J., & Marian, V. (2013). Bilingual memory: structure, access, and processing. In: Altarriba, J., & Isurin, L. (Eds.). *Memory, language, and bilingualism: theoretical and applied approaches*. Cambridge University Press.

Bear, A., & Rand, D. G. (2016). Intuition, deliberation, and the evolution of cooperation. *Proceedings of the national academy of sciences, 113*(4), 936–941.

Becker, A., Deckers, T., Dohmen, T., Falk, A., & Kosse, F. (2012). The relationship between economic preferences and psychological personality measures. *Annual review of economics, 4*(1), 453–478.

S. Nothelfer, *Behavior in Foreign Languages*, Innovation und Entrepreneurship, https://doi.org/10.1007/978-3-658-31853-6

Bernhard, H., Fehr, E., & Fischbacher, U. (2006). Group affiliation and altruistic norm enforcement. *American economic review, 96*(2), 217–221.

Bolton, G. E., & Ockenfels, A. (2000). ERC: A theory of equity, reciprocity, and competition. *American economic review, 90*(1), 166–193.

Bond, M. H., & Lai, T. M. (1986). Embarrassment and code-switching into a second language. *Journal of social psychology, 126*(2), 179–186.

Bond, M. H., & Yang, K. S. (1982). Ethnic affirmation versus cross-cultural accommodation: The variable impact of questionnaire language on Chinese bilinguals from Hong Kong. *Journal of cross-cultural psychology, 13*(2), 169–185.

Boroditsky, L. (2001). Does language shape thought? Mandarin and English speakers' conceptions of time. *Cognitive psychology, 43*(1), 1–22.

Boroditsky, L. (2003). Linguistic Relativity. In: Nadel, L. (Ed.) *Encyclopedia of Cognitive Science.* (pp. 917–921). London: MacMillan Press.

Bouwmeester, S., Verkoeijen, P. P., Aczel, B., Barbosa, F., Bègue, L., Brañas-Garza, P., … & Wollbrant, C. E. (2017). Registered replication report: Rand, greene, and nowak (2012). *Perspectives on psychological science, 12*(3), 527–542.

Bowles, S., & Gintis, H. (2002). Prosocial Emotions. In L. Blume & S. N. Durlauf (eds.) *The Economy as a Evolving Complex System 3* (pp. 337–366). Oxford: Oxford University Press.

Brynjolfsson, E., & McAfee, A. (2014). The second machine age: Work, progress, and prosperity in a time of brilliant technologies. New York: WW Norton & Company.

Brynjolfsson, E., Hui, X., & Liu, M. (2018). Does Machine Translation Affect International Trade? Evidence from a Large Digital Platform. *NBER working paper no. 24917.* Retreived from: http://www.nber.org/papers/w24917.

Brislin, R. W. (1970). Back-translation for cross-cultural research. *Journal of cross-cultural psychology, 1*(3), 185–216.

Caldwell-Harris, C. L., & Ayçiçeği-Dinn, A. (2009). Emotion and lying in a non-native language. *International journal of psychophysiology, 71*(3), 193–204.

Chaudhuri, A. (2011). Sustaining cooperation in laboratory public goods experiments: a selective survey of the literature. *Experimental economics, 14*(1), 47–83.

Chen, M. K. (2013). The effect of language on economic behavior: Evidence from savings rates, health behaviors, and retirement assets. *The american economic review, 103*(2), 690–731.

Chen, D. L., Schonger, M., & Wickens, C. (2016). oTree—An open-source platform for laboratory, online, and field experiments. *Journal of behavioral and experimental Finance, 9*, 88–97.

Church, A. T., Katigbak, M. S., & Castaneda, I. (1988). The effects of language of data collection on derived conceptions of healthy personality with Filipino bilinguals. *Journal of cross-cultural psychology, 19*(2), 178–192.

Cipolletti, H., McFarlane, S., & Weissglass, C. (2016). The moral foreign-language effect. *Philosophical psychology, 29*(1), 23–40.

Costa, A., Foucart, A., Arnon, I., Aparici, M., & Apesteguia, J. (2014a). "Piensa" twice: on the foreign language effect in decision making. *Cognition, 130*(2), 236–254.

Costa, A., Foucart, A., Hayakawa, S., Aparici, M., Apesteguia, J., Heafner, J., & Keysar, B. (2014b). Your morals depend on language. *PloS one, 9*(4), e94842.

Corey, J. D., Hayakawa, S., Foucart, A., Aparici, M., Botella, J., Costa, A., & Keysar, B. (2017). Our moral choices are foreign to us. *Journal of experimental psychology: learning, memory, and cognition*, *43*(7), 1109.

Csikszentmihalyi, M. (2014). *The Systems Model of Creativity*. Berlin: Springer.

Csikszentmihalyi, M., & Getzels, J. W. (1971). Discovery-oriented behavior and the originality of creative products: A study with artists. *Journal of personality and social psychology, 19*(1), 47.

Cubitt, R. P., Drouvelis, M., Gächter, S., & Kabalin, R. (2011). Moral judgments in social dilemmas: How bad is free riding? *Journal of public economics*, *95*(3–4), 253–264.

Dahan, E., Mendelson, H. (2001). An Extreme-Value Model of Concept Testing. *Management science, 47*(1), 102–116.

Dawes, R. M., & Thaler, R. H. (1988). Anomalies: cooperation. *Journal of economic perspectives, 2*(3), 187–197.

De Dreu, C. K., Baas, M., & Nijstad, B. A. (2008). Hedonic tone and activation level in the mood-creativity link: toward a dual pathway to creativity model. *Journal of personality and social psychology*, *94*(5), 739.

De Hooge, I. E., Zeelenberg, M., & Breugelmans, S. M. (2007). Moral sentiments and cooperation: Differential influences of shame and guilt. *Cognition and emotion*, *21*(5), 1025–1042.

Dewaele, J. M. (2004). The emotional force of swearwords and taboo words in the speech of multilinguals. *Journal of multilingual and multicultural development*, *25*(2–3), 204–222.

Dewaele, J. (2010). *Emotions in multiple languages*. New York: Palgrave Macmillan.

Dorrough, A. R., & Glöckner, A. (2016). Multinational investigation of cross-societal cooperation. *Proceedings of the national academy of sciences*, *113*(39), 10836–10841.

Dosi, G. (1988). Sources, procedures, and microeconomic effects of innovation. *Journal of economic literature, 26*(3), 1120–1171.

Dufwenberg, M., Gächter, S., & Hennig-Schmidt, H. (2011). The framing of games and the psychology of play. *Games and economic behavior*, *73*(2), 459–478.

Dufwenberg, M., & Kirchsteiger, G. (2004). A theory of sequential reciprocity. *Games and economic behavior*, *47*(2), 268–298.

Duncker, K. & Lees, L. S. (1945). On problem solving. *Psychological monographs, 58*(5).

Earle, M. J. (1969). A cross-cultural and cross-language comparison of dogmatism scores. *The journal of social psychology*, *79*(1), 19–24.

European Commission (2013). *Frequently asked questions on languages in Europe*. Press release, IP/13/875. Retreived from http://europa.eu/.

Everett, C. (2013). Linguistic relativity: Evidence across languages and cognitive domains. Berlin: Walter de Gruyter.

Fehr, E., & Schmidt, K. M. (1999). A theory of fairness, competition, and cooperation. *The quarterly journal of economics*, *114*(3), 817–868.

Fehr, E., & Fischbacher, U. (2004). Social norms and human cooperation. *Trends in cognitive sciences*, *8*(4), 185–190.

Fiedler, S., Hellmann, D. M., Dorrough, A. R., & Glöckner, A. (2018). Cross-national in-group favoritism in prosocial behavior: Evidence from Latin and North America. *Judgment & decision making*, *13*(1), 42–60.

Finke, R. A., Ward, T. M., & Smith, S. M. (1992). *Creative cognition: theory, research, and applications*. Cambridge, MA: MIT Press.

Fischbacher, U., & Föllmi-Heusi, F. (2013). Lies in disguise—an experimental study on cheating. *Journal of the european economic association, 11*(3), 525–547.

Fischbacher, U., & Gächter, S. (2010). Social preferences, beliefs, and the dynamics of free riding in public goods experiments. *American economic review, 100*(1), 541–56.

Fischbacher, U., Gächter, S., & Fehr, E. (2001). Are people conditionally cooperative? Evidence from a public goods experiment. *Economics letters, 71*(3), 397–404.

Fong, C. T. (2006). The effects of emotional ambivalence on creativity. *Academy of management journal, 49*(5), 1016–1030.

Gächter, S., & Herrmann, B. (2009). Reciprocity, culture and human cooperation: previous insights and a new cross-cultural experiment. *Philosophical transactions of the royal society of london b: biological sciences, 364*(1518), 791–806.

Gächter, S., Herrmann, B., & Thöni, C. (2010). Culture and cooperation. *Philosophical transactions of the royal society of london b: biological sciences, 365*(1553), 2651–2661.

Gargalianou, V., Urbig, D., & van Witteloostuijn, A. (2017). Cooperating or competing in three languages: cultural accommodation or alienation? *Cross cultural & strategic management, 24*(1), 167–191.

Geipel, J., Hadjichristidis, C., & Surian, L. (2015). How foreign language shapes moral judgment. *Journal of experimental social psychology, 59*, 8–17.

Geipel, J., Hadjichristidis, C., & Surian, L. (2016). Foreign language affects the contribution of intentions and outcomes to moral judgment. *Cognition, 154*, 34–39.

George, J. M., & Zhou, J. (2002). Understanding when bad moods foster creativity and good ones don't: the role of context and clarity of feelings. *Journal of applied psychology, 87*(4), 687.

Gick, M. L., & Holyoak, K. J. (1980). Analogical problem solving. *Cognitive psychology, 12*(3), 306–355.

Girotra, K., Terwiesch, C., & Ulrich, K. T. (2010). Idea Generation and the Quality of the Best Idea. *Management science, 56*(4), 591–605.

Haans, R. F. J., & Van Witteloostuijn, A. (2017). Does foreign language liberate or limit creativity? In: Haans, R. F. J. (2017): *Disentangling novelty and usefulness*. (Doctoral dissertation, Tilburg University, The Netherlands). Retrieved from https://pure.uvt.nl/portal/en/publications/disentangling-novelty-and-usefulness(66bdb7c9-5b7b-4c29-b73b-19dee434f505).html.

Hadjichristidis, C., Geipel, J., & Savadori, L. (2015). The effect of foreign language in judgments of risk and benefit: The role of affect. *Journal of experimental psychology: applied, 21*(2), 117.

Harris, C. L., Aycicegi, A., & Gleason, J. B. (2003). Taboo words and reprimands elicit greater autonomic reactivity in a first language than in a second language. *Applied psycholinguistics, 24*(4), 561–579.

Harzing, A. W., & Maznevski, M. (2002). The interaction between language and culture: A test of the cultural accommodation hypothesis in seven countries. *Language and intercultural communication, 2*(2), 120–139.

Hayakawa, S., Tannenbaum, D., Costa, A., Corey, J. D., & Keysar, B. (2017). Thinking more or feeling less? Explaining the foreign-language effect on moral judgment. *Psychological science, 28*(10), 1387–1397.

Hirt, E. R., Devers, E. E., & McCrea, S. M. (2008). I want to be creative: exploring the role of hedonic contingency theory in the positive mood-cognitive flexibility link. *Journal of personality and social psychology, 94*(2), 214.

Hoffman, E., McCabe, K., & Smith, V. L. (1996). Social distance and other-regarding behavior in dictator games. *The american economic review, 86*(3), 653–660.

Hofstede, G. (1991). Cultures and Organizations: Software of the Mind. New York: McGraw-Hill.

Hofstede, G. (2011). Dimensionalizing cultures: The Hofstede model in context. *Online readings in psychology and culture, 2*(1), 8.

Hofstede, G. (2018, July 4). *Country Comparison Tool.* Retrieved from https://www.hofstede-insights.com/product/compare-countries/.

Inglehart, R., & Baker, W. E. (2000). Modernization, cultural change, and the persistence of traditional values. *American sociological review 65*, 19–51.

Isen, A. M., Daubman, K. A., & Nowicki, G. P. (1987). Positive affect facilitates creative problem solving. *Journal of personality and social psychology, 52*(6), 1122.

January, D., & Kako, E. (2007). Re-evaluating evidence for linguistic relativity: Reply to Boroditsky (2001). *Cognition, 104*(2), 417–426.

Kahneman, D. (2003). A perspective on judgment and choice: mapping bounded rationality. *American psychologist, 58*(9), 697.

Kahneman, D. (2011). *Thinking, fast and slow.* New York: Farrar, Straus and Giroux.

Kaufman, J. C., Baer, J., & Cole, J. C. (2009). Expertise, domains, and the consensual assessment technique. *Journal of creative behavior, 43*(4), 223–233.

Kaufman, G., & Vosburg, S. (1997). 'Paradoxical' Mood Effects on Creative Problem-solving. *Cognition & emotion, 11*(2), 151–170.

Kaufman, J. C., & Sternberg, R. J. (Eds.). (2006). *The International Handbook of Creativity.* Cambridge: Cambridge University Press.

Kay, P., & Kempton, W. (1984). What is the Sapir-Whorf hypothesis? *American anthropologist, 86(1), 65–79.*

Ketelaar, T., & Tung Au, W. (2003). The effects of feelings of guilt on the behaviour of uncooperative individuals in repeated social bargaining games: An affect-as-information interpretation of the role of emotion in social interaction. *Cognition and emotion, 17*(3), 429–453.

Keysar, B., Hayakawa, S. L., & An, S. G. (2012). The foreign-language effect: Thinking in a foreign tongue reduces decision biases. *Psychological science, 23*(6), 661–668.

Kocher, M. G., Cherry, T., Kroll, S., Netzer, R. J., & Sutter, M. (2008). Conditional cooperation on three continents. *Economics letters, 101*(3), 175–178.

Kroll, J. F., & Tokowicz, N. (2005). Models of bilingual representation and processing: Looking back and to the future. In: Kroll, J. F., & De Groot, A. (Eds.). *Handbook of bilingualism: psycholinguistic approaches.* New York: Oxford University Press.

Krupka, E. L., & Weber, R. A. (2013). Identifying social norms using coordination games: Why does dictator game sharing vary? *Journal of the european economic association, 11*(3), 495–524.

Laske, K., & Schröder, M. (2017). Quantity, Quality and Originality: The Effects of Incentives on Creativity. Beiträge zur jahrestagung des vereins für socialpolitik 2017: alternative geld- und finanzarchitekturen, no. B01-V3.

Ledyard, J. (1995). Public Goods: A Survey of Experimental Research. in J. H. Kagel & A. E. Roth (eds.), *Handbook of experimental economics*. Princeton, NJ: Princeton University Press.

Leung, A. K. Y., Maddux, W. W., Galinsky, A. D., & Chiu, C. Y. (2008). Multicultural experience enhances creativity: the when and how. *American psychologist*, *63*(3), 169–181.

Li, K. K. (2017). How does language affect decision-making in social interactions and decision biases? *Journal of economic psychology*, *61*, 15–28.

Lüsebrink, H. J. (2005). *Interkulturelle Kommunikation*. Stuttgart: J.B. Metzler.

Maddux, W. W., & Galinsky, A. D. (2009). Cultural borders and mental barriers: the relationship between living abroad and creativity. *Journal of personality and social psychology*, *96*(5), 1047–1061.

Marian, V., Kaushanskaya, M., 2004. Language-mediated self-construal and emotion in bicultural bilinguals. *Journal of memory and language 51*, 190–201.

Marian, V., & Neisser, U. (2000). Language-dependent recall of autobiographical memories. *Journal of experimental psychology: general*, *129*(3), 361–368.

Mednick, S. (1962). The associative basis of the creative process. *Psychological review*, *69*(3), 220–232.

Morford, J. P., Wilkinson, E., Villwock, A., Piñar, P., & Kroll, J. F. (2011). When deaf signers read English: Do written words activate their sign translations? *Cognition*, *118*(2), 286–292.

Neeley, T. (2012). Global business speaks English. *Harvard business review*, *90*, 116–124.

Niu, W., & Sternberg, R. J. (2001). Cultural influences on artistic creativity and its evaluation. *International journal of psychology*, *36*(4), 225–241.

Nothelfer, S. (2017). *Foreign Language Effects on Creativity* (Unpublished MBR Project Study). Ludwig-Maximilians-Universität München, Germany.

Obmann, C. (2017, September 26). Lost without Translation. *Handelsblatt*. Retrieved from https://www.handelsblatt.com.

Oosterbeek, H., Sloof, R., & Van De Kuilen, G. (2004). Cultural differences in ultimatum game experiments: Evidence from a meta-analysis. *Experimental economics*, *7*(2), 171–188.

Ostrom, E., & Walker, J. (1991). Communication in a commons: cooperation without external enforcement. In: Palfrey, T. R. (ed.). *Laboratory research in political economy*, 287–322. Ann-Arbor, MI: University of Michigan Press.

Ostrom, E., Walker, J., & Gardner, R. (1992). Covenants with and without a sword: Self-governance is possible. *American political science review*, *86*(2), 404–417.

Pavlenko, A. (2005). *Emotions and Mulitilingualism*. New York, NY: Cambridge University Press.

Penn, J. M. (2014). *Linguistic relativity versus innate ideas: The origins of the Sapir-Whorf hypothesis in German thought*. Berlin: Walter de Gruyter.

Plucker, J. A., & Makel, M. C. (2010). Assessment of creativity. In: Kaufman, J. & Sternberg, R. (Eds.). *The Cambridge handbook of creativity*. (pp. 48–73). New York, NY: Cambridge University Press.

Pütz, M., & Verspoor, M. (Eds.). (2000). *Explorations in linguistic relativity*. Amsterdam: John Benjamins Publishing.
Rand, D. G., Greene, J. D., & Nowak, M. A. (2012). Spontaneous giving and calculated greed. *Nature, 489*(7416), 427–430.
Rabin, M. (1993). Incorporating fairness into game theory and economics. *The American economic review*, 1281–1302.
Runco, M. A. (Ed.). (1994). *Problem finding, problem solving, and creativity*. Norwood, NJ: Ablex Publishing Company.
Runco, M. A. (2007). Creativity: Theories and Themes: Research, Development, and Practice. Burlington, MA: Elsevier.
Schrauf, R. W., & Rubin, D. C. (1998). Bilingual autobiographical memory in older adult immigrants: A test of cognitive explanations of the reminiscence bump and the linguistic encoding of memories. *Journal of memory and language, 39*(3), 437–457.
Schrauf, R. W., & Rubin, D. C. (2000). Internal languages of retrieval: The bilingual encoding of memories for the personal past. *Memory & cognition, 28*(4), 616–623.
Shook, A., & Marian, V. (2012). Bimodal bilinguals co-activate both languages during spoken comprehension. *Cognition, 124*(3), 314–324.
Shook, A., & Marian, V. (2013). The bilingual language interaction network for comprehension of speech. *Bilingualism: language and cognition, 16*(2), 304–324.
Shrout, P. E., & Fleiss, J. L. (1979). Intraclass correlations: uses in assessing rater reliability. *Psychological bulletin, 86*(2), 420–428.
Simons, G. F., & Fennig, C. D. (Eds.). (2018). *Ethnologue: Languages of the world (21st ed.)*. Dallas, TX: SIL International. Online version: http://www.ethnologue.com.
Simonton, D. K. (2004). *Creativity in science: Chance, Logic, Genius, and Zeitgeist*. New York, NY: Cambridge University Press.
Sutter, M., Angerer, S., Rützler, D., & Lergetporer, P. (2015). The Effect of Language on Economic Behavior: Experimental Evidence from Children's Intertemporal Choices. *Discussion paper.* IZA DP No. 9383.
Sternberg, R. J., & Lubart, T. I. (1996). Investing in creativity. *American psychologist, 51*(7), 677–688.
Szmalec, A., Brysbaert, M., & Duyck, W. (2012). Working memory and (second) language processing. In *Memory, language, and bilingualism: theoretical and applied approaches* (pp. 74–94). New York, NY: Cambridge University Press.
Tinghög, G., Andersson, D., Bonn, C., Böttiger, H., Josephson, C., Lundgren, G., … & Johannesson, M. (2013). Intuition and cooperation reconsidered. *Nature, 498*(7452).
United Nations (2018, September 12). *Official Languages*. Retreived from: http://www.un.org/en/sections/about-un/official-languages/.
Urbig, D., Terjesen, S., Procher, V., Muehlfeld, K., & Van Witteloostuijn, A. (2016). Come on and take a free ride: Contributing to public goods in native and foreign language settings. *Academy of management learning & education, 15*(2), 268–286.
Van Hugten, J., & Van Witteloostuijn, A. (2018). The foreign language effect on the self-serving bias: A field experiment in the high school classroom. *PloS one, 13*(2), e0192143.
W3Techs (2018, September 6). Web Technology Surveys: Usage of content languages for websites. Retrieved from https://w3techs.com/.

Wahl, L. M., & Nowak, M. A. (1999). The continuous Prisoner's Dilemma: I. Linear reactive strategies. *Journal of theoretical biology, 200*(3), 307–321.

Ward, T. B. (2004). Cognition, creativity, and entrepreneurship. *Journal of business venturing, 19*(2), 173–188.

West, M. A., & Anderson, N. R. (1996). Innovation in top management teams. *Journal of applied psychology, 81*(6), 680–693.

Wong, R. Y. M., & Hong, Y. Y. (2005). Dynamic influences of culture on cooperation in the prisoner's dilemma. *Psychological science, 16*(6), 429–434.

Wu, Y. J., & Thierry, G. (2012a). How reading in a second language protects your heart. *Journal of neuroscience, 32*(19), 6485–6489.

Wu, Y. J., & Thierry, G. (2012b). Unconscious translation during incidental foreign language processing. *Neuroimage, 59*(4), 3468–3473.

Yang, K. S., & Bond, M. H. (1980). Ethnic affirmation by Chinese bilinguals. *Journal of cross-cultural psychology, 11*(4), 411–425.

Zaki, J., & Mitchell, J. P. (2013). Intuitive prosociality. *Current directions in psychological science, 22*(6), 466–470.

Zelmer, J. (2003). Linear public goods experiments: A meta-analysis. *Experimental economics, 6*(3), 299–310.